Word Association Thematic Analysis

A Social Media Text Exploration Strategy

Synthesis Lectures on Information Concepts, Retrieval, and Services

Synthesis Lectures on Information Concepts, Retrieval, and Services publishes short books on topics pertaining to information science and applications of technology to information discovery, production, distribution, and management. Potential topics include: data models, indexing theory and algorithms, classification, information architecture, information economics, privacy and identity, scholarly communication, bibliometrics and webometrics, personal information management, human information behavior, digital libraries, archives and preservation, cultural informatics, information retrieval evaluation, data fusion, relevance feedback, recommendation systems, question answering, natural language processing for retrieval, text summarization, multimedia retrieval, multilingual retrieval, and exploratory search.

Word Association Thematic Analysis: A Social Media Text Exploration Strategy
Michael Thelwall

Simulating Information Retrieval Test Collections
David Hawking, Bodo Billerbeck, Paul Thomas, and Nick Craswell

Automatic Disambiguation of Author Names in Bibliographic Repositories
Anderson A. Ferreira, Marcos André Gonçalves, and Alberto H. F. Laender

Compatibility Modeling: Data and Knowledge Applications for Clothing Matching
Xuemeng Song, Liqiang Nie, and Yinglong Wang

Video Structure Meaning
Brian C. O'Connor and Richard L. Anderson

Interactive IR User Study Design, Evaluation, and Reporting
Jiqun Liu and Chirag Shah

The Practice of Crowdsourcing
Omar Alonso

Predicting Information Retrieval Performance
Robert M. Losee

Framing Privacy in Digital Collections with Ethical Decision Making
Virginia Dressler

Mobile Search Behaviors: An In-depth Analysis Based on Contexts, APPs, and Devices
Dan Wu and Shaobo Liang

Images in Social Media: Categorization and Organization of Images and Their Collections
Susanne Ørnager and Haakon Lund

Exploring Context in Information Behavior: Seeker, Situation, Surroundings, and Shared Identities
Naresh Kumar Agarwal

Researching Serendipity in Digital Information Environments
Lori McCay-Peet and Elaine G. Toms

Social Monitoring for Public Health
Michael J. Paul and Mark Dredze

Digital Libraries for Cultural Heritage: Development, Outcomes, and Challenges from European Perspectives
Tatjana Aparac-Jelušić

iRODS Primer 2: Integrated Rule-Oriented Data System
Hao Xu, Terrell Russell, Jason Coposky, Arcot Rajasekar, Reagan Moore, Antoine de Torcy, Michael Wan, Wayne Shroeder, and Sheau-Yen Chen

Information Architecture: The Design and Integration of Information Spaces, Second Edition
Wei Ding, Xia Lin, and Michael Zarro

Fuzzy Information Retrieval
Donald H. Kraft and Erin Colvin

Quantifying Research Integrity
Michael Seadle

Incidental Exposure to Online News
Borchuluun Yadamsuren and Sanda Erdelez

Web Indicators for Research Evaluation: A Practical Guide
Michael Thelwall

Trustworthy Policies for Distributed Repositories
Reagan W. Moore, Hao Xu, Mike Conway, Arcot Rajasekar, Jon Crabtree, and Helen Tibbo

The Notion of Relevance in Information Science: Everybody knows what relevance is. But, what is it really?
Tefko Saracevic

Dynamic Information Retrieval Modeling
Grace Hui Yang, Marc Sloan, and Jun Wang

Learning from Multiple Social Networks
Liqiang Nie, Xuemeng Song, and Tat-Seng Chua

Scholarly Collaboration on the Academic Social Web
Daqing He and Wei Jeng

Scalability Challenges in Web Search Engines
B. Barla Cambazoglu and Ricardo Baeza-Yates

Social Informatics Evolving
Pnina Fichman, Madelyn R. Sanfilippo, and Howard Rosenbaum

On the Efficient Determination of Most Near Neighbors: Horseshoes, Hand Grenades, Web Search and Other Situations When Close Is Close Enough, Second Edition
Mark S. Manasse

Building a Better World with Our Information: The Future of Personal Information Management, Part 3
William Jones

Click Models for Web Search
Aleksandr Chuklin, Ilya Markov, and Maarten de Rijke

Information Communication
Feicheng Ma

Social Media and Library Services
Lorraine Mon

Analysis and Visualization of Citation Networks
Dangzhi Zhao and Andreas Strotmann

The Taxobook: Applications, Implementation, and Integration in Search, Part 3
Marjorie M. K. Hlava

The Taxobook: Principles and Practices of Building Taxonomies, Part 2
Marjorie M. K. Hlava

Measuring User Engagement
Mounia Lalmas, Heather O'Brien, and Elad Yom-Tov

The Taxobook: History, Theories, and Concepts of *Knowledge Organization*, Part 1
Marjorie M. K. Hlava

Children's Internet Search: Using Roles to Understand Children's Search Behavior
Elizabeth Foss and Allison Druin

Digital Library Technologies: Complex Objects, Annotation, Ontologies, Classification, Extraction, and Security
Edward A. Fox and Ricardo da Silva Torres

Digital Libraries Applications: CBIR, Education, Social Networks, eScience/Simulation, and GIS
Edward A. Fox and Jonathan P. Leidig

Information and Human Values
Kenneth R. Fleischmann

Multiculturalism and Information and Communication Technology
Pnina Fichman and Madelyn R. Sanfilippo

Transforming Technologies to Manage Our Information: The Future of Personal Information Management, Part II
William Jones

Designing for Digital Reading
Jennifer Pearson, George Buchanan, and Harold Thimbleby

Information Retrieval Models: Foundations and Relationships
Thomas Roelleke

Key Issues Regarding Digital Libraries: Evaluation and Integration
Rao Shen, Marcos Andre Goncalves, and Edward A. Fox

Visual Information Retrieval Using Java and LIRE
Mathias Lux and Oge Marques

On the Efficient Determination of Most Near Neighbors: Horseshoes, Hand Grenades, Web Search and Other Situations When Close is Close Enough
Mark S. Manasse

The Answer Machine
Susan E. Feldman

Theoretical Foundations for Digital Libraries: The 5S (Societies, Scenarios, Spaces, Structures, Streams) Approach
Edward A. Fox, Marcos André Gonçalves, and Rao Shen

The Future of Personal Information Management, Part I: Our Information, Always and Forever
William Jones

Search User Interface Design
Max L. Wilson

Information Retrieval Evaluation
Donna Harman

Knowledge Management (KM) Processes in Organizations: Theoretical Foundations and Practice
Claire R. McInerney and Michael E. D. Koenig

Search-Based Applications: At the Confluence of Search and Database Technologies
Gregory Grefenstette and Laura Wilber

Information Concepts: From Books to Cyberspace Identities
Gary Marchionini

Estimating the Query Difficulty for Information Retrieval
David Carmel and Elad Yom-Tov

iRODS Primer: Integrated Rule-Oriented Data System
Arcot Rajasekar, Reagan Moore, Chien-Yi Hou, Christopher A. Lee, Richard Marciano, Antoine de Torcy, Michael Wan, Wayne Schroeder, Sheau-Yen Chen, Lucas Gilbert, Paul Tooby, and Bing Zhu

Collaborative Web Search: Who, What, Where, When, and Why
Meredith Ringel Morris and Jaime Teevan

Multimedia Information Retrieval
Stefan Rüger

Online Multiplayer Games
William Sims Bainbridge

Information Architecture: The Design and Integration of Information Spaces
Wei Ding and Xia Lin

Reading and Writing the Electronic Book
Catherine C. Marshall

Hypermedia Genes: An Evolutionary Perspective on Concepts, Models, and Architectures
Nuno M. Guimarães and Luís M. Carrico

Understanding User-Web Interactions via Web Analytics
Bernard J. (Jim) Jansen

XML Retrieval
Mounia Lalmas

Faceted Search
Daniel Tunkelang

Introduction to Webometrics: Quantitative Web Research for the Social Sciences
Michael Thelwall

Exploratory Search: Beyond the Query-Response Paradigm
Ryen W. White and Resa A. Roth

New Concepts in Digital Reference
R. David Lankes

Automated Metadata in Multimedia Information Systems: Creation, Refinement, Use in Surrogates, and Evaluation
Michael G. Christel

Word Association Thematic Analysis: A Social Media Text Exploration Strategy
Michael Thelwall

www.morganclaypool.com

ISBN: 9781636390659 print
ISBN: 9781636390666 ebook
ISBN: 9781636390673 hardcover

DOI 10.2200/S01071ED1V01Y202012ICR072

A Publication in the Morgan and Claypool Publishers series
SYNTHESIS LECTURES ON INFORMATION CONCEPTS, RETRIEVAL, AND SERVICES
Lecture #72
Series Editor: Gary Marchionini, University of North Carolina at Chapel Hill

Series ISSN 1947-945X Print 1947-9468 Electronic

Word Association Thematic Analysis

A Social Media Text Exploration Strategy

Michael Thelwall
University of Wolverhampton

SYNTHESIS LECTURES ON INFORMATION CONCEPTS, RETRIEVAL, AND SERVICES #72

MORGAN & CLAYPOOL PUBLISHERS

ABSTRACT

Many research projects involve analyzing sets of texts from the social web or elsewhere to get insights into issues, opinions, interests, news discussions, or communication styles. For example, many studies have investigated reactions to Covid-19 social distancing restrictions, conspiracy theories, and anti-vaccine sentiment on social media. This book describes word association thematic analysis, a mixed methods strategy to identify themes within a collection of social web or other texts. It identifies these themes in the differences between subsets of the texts, including female vs. male vs. nonbinary, older vs. newer, country A vs. country B, positive vs. negative sentiment, high scoring vs. low scoring, or subtopic A vs. subtopic B. It can also be used to identify the differences between a topic-focused collection of texts and a reference collection. The method starts by automatically finding words that are statistically significantly more common in one subset than another, then identifies the context of these words and groups them into themes. It is supported by the free Windows-based software Mozdeh for data collection or importing and for the quantitative analysis stages. This book explains the word association thematic analysis method, with examples, and gives practical advice for using it. It is primarily intended for social media researchers and students, although the method is applicable to any collection of short texts.

KEYWORDS

word association, social media, thematic analysis, text analysis, statistics, data collection

Contents

Acknowledgments xv

1 Introduction 1
- 1.1 Overview: Word Association Detection, Contextualization, and Thematic Analysis 3
- 1.2 WAA and WATA Examples 5
- 1.3 Research Philosophy: Mixed Methods 7
- 1.4 Comparison with Traditional Social Research Methods 8
- 1.5 Software: Mozdeh 10
- 1.6 Language and International Considerations 11
- 1.7 Using This Book 11

2 Data Collection with Mozdeh 13
- 2.1 Sample Size 13
- 2.2 Data Collection Methods 13
  - 2.2.1 Query-Based Post Collection (Twitter) 13
  - 2.2.2 User-Based Post Collection (Twitter, YouTube) 15
  - 2.2.3 User Profile Bio Collection (Twitter) 16
  - 2.2.4 Other Methods to Identify a Set of Texts for Analysis 16
- 2.3 Mozdeh Data Collection Procedures 16
  - 2.3.1 Query-Based Post Collection in Mozdeh 17
  - 2.3.2 User-Based Post Collection with Mozdeh 19
  - 2.3.3 User Profile Bio Collection with Mozdeh 19
  - 2.3.4 Importing Text Collections (Academic Publications, Other) into Mozdeh 19
- 2.4 Filtering the Initial Dataset 21
- 2.5 Summary 21

3 Word Association Detection: Term Identification 23
- 3.1 Word Association Detection: Subset vs. the Rest 24
  - 3.1.1 Choice of Comparator Set 25
  - 3.1.2 Word Association Detection with Mozdeh 26
- 3.2 Word Association Detection: Subset A vs. Subset B 30

3.3 Statistical Details . . . 33
3.3.1 Theoretical Assumptions . . . 35
3.3.2 Effect Sizes . . . 36
3.4 Protection Against Accidentally Finding Irrelevant Words . . . 37
3.5 Sample Size Requirements . . . 37
3.6 Limitations . . . 37
3.7 Summary . . . 38

4 Word Association Contextualization: Term Meaning and Context . . . 41
4.1 Word Association Contextualization from a Random Sample of Relevant Texts . . . 43
4.1.1 Word Association Contextualization Overview . . . 43
4.1.2 Creating the WAC Text Sample with Mozdeh . . . 44
4.1.3 Detecting Typical Meanings for Polysemous Words and Words in Expressions . . . 47
4.1.4 Identifying Word Contexts . . . 48
4.1.5 Difficult Cases: Pronouns and Stylistic Words . . . 49
4.1.6 Random Sample Summary . . . 50
4.2 Advanced Word Association Contextualization . . . 52
4.2.1 Follow-Up Word Association Detection for the Term . . . 52
4.2.2 Follow-Up Word Association Detection Within Texts Containing the Term . . . 54
4.3 Word Association Contextualization Test Assumptions . . . 56
4.4 Causes of Word Associations: News, Viral Sharing, or Societal Differences? . . . 57
4.5 Using Multiple Coders . . . 58
4.6 Reporting WAA . . . 59
4.7 Summary . . . 59

5 Word Association Thematic Analysis: Theme Detection . . . 61
5.1 Assigning Themes to Words . . . 61
5.2 WATA Procedure . . . 62
5.3 WATA Visual and Performing Arts Example . . . 64
5.4 Using Multiple Coders . . . 69
5.5 Reporting WATA . . . 69
5.5.1 Theme Prevalence Information . . . 70
5.5.2 Discussing the Results . . . 72
5.6 Summary . . . 72

6 Word Association Thematic Analysis Examples **75**

6.1 Gender Differences in Early Covid-19 Tweeting 75

6.2 Gender Differences in Museum Comments on YouTube 81

6.3 Gender Differences in Academic Publishing 84

6.4 International Differences in Academic Nursing Publishing 87

6.5 Summary 89

7 Comparison Between WATA and Other Methods **91**

7.1 Content Analysis 91

7.2 Thematic Analysis 92

7.3 Word Clouds 92

7.4 Top Hashtags 93

7.5 Document Clustering 93

7.6 Document Set Mapping 93

7.7 Topic Modeling 93

7.8 Text/Semantic Networks 94

7.9 Natural Language Processing and Pre-Processing Possibilities 95

7.10 Corpus-Assisted Critical Discourse Analysis 96

7.11 Summary 97

8 Ethics **99**

8.1 Is Permission Required to Analyze Public Texts? 99

8.2 Can Posters Be Named or Quoted? 100

8.3 Summary 100

9 Project Planning **101**

10 Summary **103**

References **105**

Author Biography **111**

Acknowledgments

Thank you to Professor Stephanie W. Haas of the University of North Carolina School of Information and Library Science and Professor Han Woo Park of the Department of Media and Communication at YeungNam University for very helpful comments on an earlier version of this book.

CHAPTER 1

Introduction

Many social science researchers analyze sets of texts to detect themes relevant to their research goals. In politics, they might identify the main topics discussed by the supporters of a new Spanish left-wing political party, international environmental activist group, or U.S.-based vaccine conspiracy theory. Health scientists might investigate how patients with asthma in Nigeria share information about it, or whether misinformation about asthma in India is shared online. In media and communication studies, the objective might be to investigate reactions to an environmental disaster or to identify gendered communication styles. In marketing, a project might identify the aspects of tourist attractions in India evaluated by visitors in online TripAdvisor reviews. While there are many existing research methods that can help these projects to find themes, the method introduced in this book explores gender, nationality, sentiment, popularity, or topic differences within the texts to identify themes in a way that is supported by statistical tests, as conducted automatically by the supporting software, and gives more fine-grained results than common existing methods.

This book describes two methods to identify themes in collections of texts from the social web or elsewhere. The texts might be sets of tweets about Covid-19, comments on YouTube videos posted by prominent fashion bloggers, posts to a sports discussion forum, journal article abstracts, news articles, TripAdvisor reviews, or another collection of short texts. The two methods described in this book are word association analysis (WAA) and word association thematic analysis (WATA). The standard WAA method identifies a set of words indicating differences in the set of texts. For example, it might find that the word *cosplay* was more tweeted by females than males in a set of manga tweets, indicating a gender difference in this aspect of manga fandom. WATA includes a follow-up identification of themes in WAA results when there are too many words to report individually. For example, in a set of manga tweets, one theme might be that fighting-related words are more used by male manga fans on Twitter. WATA is a large sample extension of WAA because each theme consists of one or more words identified by the first method. These methods are supported by the free Windows-based software Mozdeh (http://mozeh.wlv.ac.uk).

The two methods both work by identifying differences between subsets of the texts, as specified by the researcher, including the following.

- **Gender:** Which issues tend to be discussed more by males, females, or nonbinary people? (Nonbinary genders are currently only identifiable from tweets for technical reasons.)

- **Country:** Which issues tend to be discussed more in one country than another (sharing a common language)?
- **Popularity:** Which issues are the most or least successful (e.g., as reflected by retweet counts)?
- **Sentiment:** Which issues generate the most positivity or negativity?
- **Time:** Which issues were discussed most during a given period, such as in the first or last documents?
- **Subtopics:** Which issues were discussed more within a given subtopic (e.g., the care home subtopic within Covid-19 tweets)?
- **Topic/reference set:** Which issues were discussed more within the topic than in a reference set (e.g., what characterizes political tweets compared to general tweets)?

The word association methods center on a comparison between two sets of texts or between two parts of a text collection, but they are also suitable for text-based research projects that do not center on comparisons. This is because they can give general insights into the topics discussed using the last method above: comparison with a reference set. For example, an investigation into how people with Attention Deficit Hyperactivity Disorder (ADHD) discussed their condition on Twitter compared their tweets to the tweets of people discussing other conditions to identify ADHD-specific themes. This study gave additional insights compared to a standard thematic analysis of the same ADHD tweets that did not contrast them with a reference set (Thelwall et al., 2021).

This book is for researchers and social media students that wish to analyze issues in the social web or other short text document collections. The goal might be to analyze an issue *indirectly* through the available social web or other documents or to analyze the social web itself *directly* through posts. Using the ADHD example above, in the first (indirect evidence) case the research question might be, "What do people with ADHD consider important about their condition?" and would be answered indirectly through social web evidence, assuming that the social web reflected the offline world to some extent. In the second (direct evidence) case, the question would focus on the social website, "How do people with ADHD tweet about their condition?" and get direct evidence from Twitter.

1.1 OVERVIEW: WORD ASSOCIATION DETECTION, CONTEXTUALIZATION, AND THEMATIC ANALYSIS

The first part of either type of project, whether WAA or WATA, is Word Association Detection (WAD). This uses the software Mozdeh to process a set of texts to find words that are statistically significantly more common in one subset of the texts than another. Here are two illustrative examples.

- Suppose that you are analyzing a set of 50,000 tweets with the hashtag #BlackLivesMatter and are investigating gender differences in tweeting about this issue. Mozdeh would produce lists of words that are more prevalent in male, female or nonbinary tweets. The result might be: Female: *structural*, *inequalities*; Male: *Trump*; *Democrat*; Nonbinary: *protest* (the lists are usually much longer).

- Suppose that you are seeking international UK vs. U.S. differences in comments posted to fashion influencer YouTube channels. For the WAD part, Mozdeh would separate the comments on U.S. YouTubers' videos from the comments on UK YouTubers' videos and produce a list of words that are more prevalent in the comments of one of either the UK or the U.S. The result might be: U.S.: *proms*, *Abercrombie*; UK: *Gents*; *leggings* (again, the lists are usually much longer).

To illustrate this further, suppose also that one of the words reported by Mozdeh as being female-associated in the #BlackLivesMatter tweets is "structural", with 2.3% of female-authored tweets containing the term compared to 1.1% of nonbinary or male-authored tweets. Although this is a small percentage difference, Mozdeh reports that it is statistically significant, so is unlikely to have occurred by chance. Lists of words and percentages are the output of the WAD stage.

The next stage is Word Association Contextualization (WAC), which involves reading texts containing each term discovered to identify its typical meaning (if it is polysemic) and context. For example, the female-associated word "structural" in the #BlackLivesMatter tweets has a dictionary definition of, "relating to the way in which parts of a system or object are arranged" (Cambridge Dictionary, 2020). In the #BlackLivesMatter tweets the context of this word is much more specific than given by the dictionary definition: it is almost always used by females to point out the structural inequalities in the system that disadvantage people because they are Black. This contextualization suggests that females are more likely to tweet about racist structural inequalities than are males or nonbinaries (male #BlackLivesMatter tweets on this topic in particular tend to be more party political). In this case, the word "inequalities" was also female associated (1.2% vs. 0.6%), for the same underlying reason that females using #BlackLivesMatter were more likely to tweet about structural inequalities than were males using #BlackLivesMatter.

WAA comprises WAD and WAC, producing lists of words that are more prevalent in one subset of the texts than another (e.g., males vs. females; nonbinary vs. male/female; earlier vs. later;

topic A vs. topic B; popular vs. unpopular; country A vs. country B; all texts vs. reference set) and short explanations of the contexts of each word:

$$\text{WAA} = \text{WAD+WAC}$$

If the WAA stage produces many terms (more than 15–25) then a Thematic Analysis (TA) extra stage is needed to group the WAA terms into coherent themes containing one or more terms that have similar meanings or contexts. The purpose of this stage is to synthesize long lists into a much shorter list of themes to help with reporting the results and to help with drawing wider conclusions from them. If the TA stage is used, then the method is called WATA:

$$\text{WATA} = \text{WAD+WAC+TA}$$

A WATA therefore has three main stages (Figure 1.1). The WAD stage is automated: After the texts are split into two or three groups (see later), the computer finds words that are more prevalent in Set A than Set B. The WAC stage is manual: a human reads appropriate texts in Set A to add context to the WAD words. The TA stage is also manual: a human organizes the contextualized words into coherent themes.

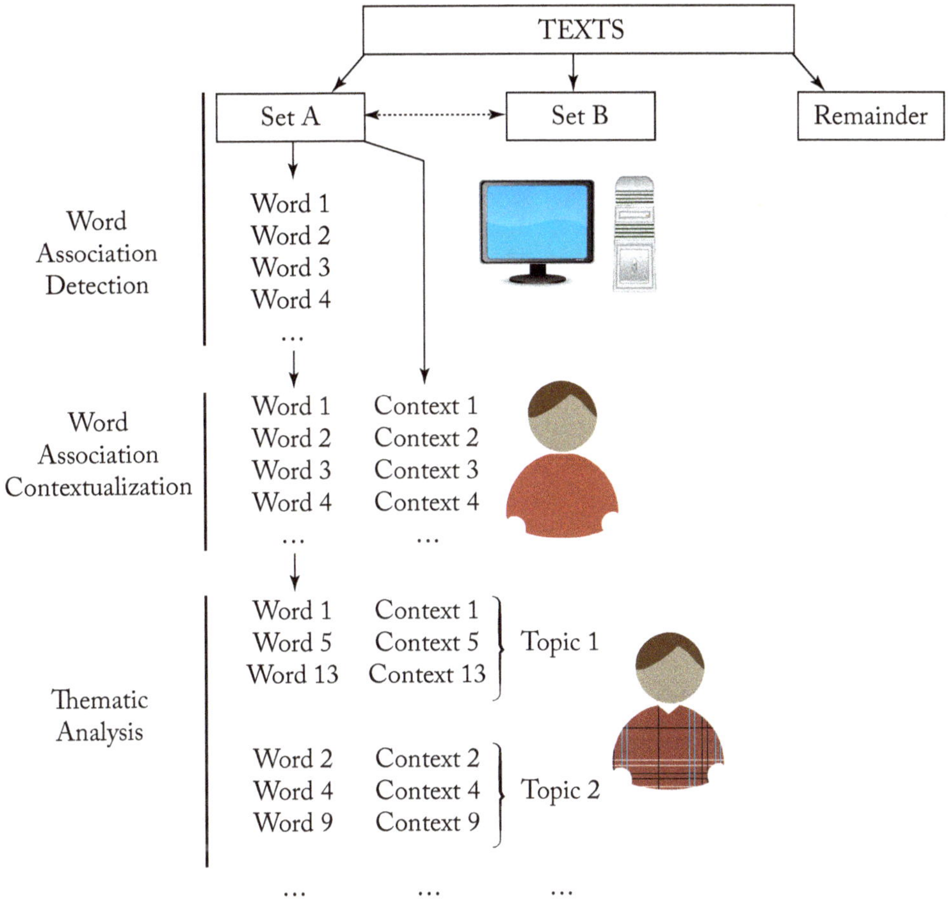

Figure 1.1: The three main stages of word association thematic analysis.

1.2 WAA AND WATA EXAMPLES

WAA studies have analyzed YouTube comments collected by Mozdeh or TripAdvisor reviews imported into Mozdeh (Table 1.1). They investigated an aspect of gender and included other types of analysis within the published article. All studies should be available free online to consult for detailed examples of the methods, although they do not name WAA explicitly.

Table 1.1: Studies using WAA

Topic	Data	Comparison	Example Findings
Gendered reactions to YouTube science videos	Comments on videos from 50 YouTube science channels	Female vs. male	Offensive gendered language is rare but directed at females (Thelwall and Mas-Bleda, 2018).
Dance	Comments on dance videos in YouTube	Female vs. male	Gendered and sentiment-associating terms for each dance style (Thelwall, 2018a).
Gender bias in sentiment analysis	TripAdvisor reviews	Female vs. male	Female hotel reviews express sentiment more explicitly (Tables 2 and 3 of Thelwall, 2018d).

WATA studies have analyzed social media (tweets, Twitter profile descriptions, YouTube comments, SteemIt, and Reddit), and academic journal article titles, abstracts, and keywords (Table 1.2). Most investigated an aspect of gender. The project about ADHD tweeting focused on a single topic, personal experiences of ADHD, rather than on any type of difference. Nevertheless, as a methodological choice, this paper compared tweets about ADHD with tweets about other disorders or diseases to discover features that were particularly prevalent for ADHD. A similar strategy was used in the paper about bullying discussions on YouTube, which contrasted them to comments on other topics. Other projects compared countries, time periods, or popularity levels. For the Twitter and YouTube projects, the program Mozdeh collected and analyzed the texts whereas for the other projects it imported them for analysis.

Table 1.2: Studies using WATA

Topic	Data	Comparison	Example Findings
Gender differences in reactions to Covid-19	Tweets mentioning Covid-19	Female vs. male	Females tweet more about safety; males more about politics (Thelwall and Thelwall, 2020).
Personal experiences of ADHD	Tweets about "my ADHD"	ADHD vs. other disorders	The brain is discussed as if it is a separate entity (Thelwall, et al., submitted).

Evolution of #BlackLivesMatter during Covid-19	Covid-19 tweets about racism	Tweets in four different periods	The George Floyd killing led to tweets about systematic racism (Thelwall and Thelwall, submitted-a).
Self-presentation on Twitter	UK Twitter profiles	Female vs. male vs. nonbinary	Nonbinary profiles more likely to mention games and sexuality (Thelwall et al., 2021).
Autism on Twitter	U.S. autism tweets during Covid-19	Autism vs. others	Autistic tweeters do not have distinctive reactions to Covid-19 (Thelwall and Thelwall, submitted).
Gender differences in museum interests	Comments on YouTube museum videos	Female vs. male	Females are more explicitly positive about content (Thelwall, 2018c).
Discussions of bullying in YouTube	Comments on YouTube influencer videos	Bullying vs. others	(Thelwall and Cash, to appear)
Interests on Reddit	Reddit posts	Female vs. male	Females more likely to mention doctors in the science subreddit (Thelwall and Stuart, 2019).
Factors associated with success in SteemIt	Steemit (like Reddit) posts	Successful vs. unsuccessful posts	Financial news is less likely to be rewarded (Thelwall, 2018b).
Nursing research	Nursing journal articles*	U.S. vs. other countries	Nursing administration and management is not studied in some countries (Thelwall and Mas-Bleda, in press).
U.S. research subjects	U.S. journal articles*	Female vs. male	Lists of gendered research topics and styles (Thelwall, et al., 2019b).
UK research subjects	UK journal articles*	Female vs. male	Lists of gendered research topics and styles (Thelwall et al., 2020).
Indian research subjects	Indian journal articles*	Female vs. male	Lists of gendered research topics and styles (Thelwall, et al., 2019a).

*Article titles, abstracts, and keywords were analyzed but not full texts.

1.3 RESEARCH PHILOSOPHY: MIXED METHODS

Word association thematic analysis uses a mixed methods research paradigm (Johnson, Onwuegbuzie, and Turner, 2007) driven by pragmatism: the need to combine both quantitative and qualitative elements sequentially to extract meaningful information from word frequencies in a set of texts. More specifically, it uses a sequential mixed methods design (Schoonenboom and Johnson, 2017) with a quantitative method followed by qualitative methods. The purpose of the qualitative methods is to explain the quantitative results, so WATA could also be classed as a two-phase explanatory mixed methods research design (Creswell, Plano Clark, Gutmann, and Hanson, 2003).

The first part of WATA involves automatically identifying words that are more common in one set of texts than another. This is purely quantitative. The software used incorporates statistical significance testing to create a set of words of interest and requires no human involvement or interpretation. Outside WATA, this approach is sometimes used for illustrative purposes, such as to create a word cloud of common words. Simple lists (or clouds) of words would not give useful information about the social context of the data or meaningful interpretations of it. They put the onus on the reader to interpret the meaning of the words identified. Someone looking at a word cloud would have to guess why the words were included and try to identify any patterns.

The second part of WATA involves human subjective judgments to identify the contexts of the words identified from the quantitative first stage and to organize the results into themes. This converts that list of words into patterns in the data that incorporate some degree of its social context. This is a qualitative approach because it involves subjective judgements and theme building.

Both the quantitative and qualitative parts of WATA are needed. Without the qualitative second part, the list of words is ambiguous and context free, giving little insight into the source of the texts. Without the quantitative first part, a qualitative analyses of words selected somehow from a set of texts would be meaningless. While other qualitative and quantitative methods can also be applied to sets of texts, this book makes the case that the WATA combination provides a useful new mixed methods approach.

1.4 COMPARISON WITH TRADITIONAL SOCIAL RESEARCH METHODS

Social research into attitudes, beliefs, and knowledge (called topics here for convenience) has traditionally used surveys, interviews, focus groups, or statistical data. Surveys and statistical data are ideal for obtaining information about large collections of people for pre-defined questions. In contrast, interviews and focus groups can be exploratory, allowing participants to introduce new ideas to the researchers. The alternative approach followed in this book is to harness texts discussing a topic from places where they already exist, such as the social web, and identify important themes. This strategy has both advantages and disadvantages compared to the others. Its main advantages are data collection speed and large sample size. Its main disadvantages are the restriction to the topics discussed in the documents analyzed and the possibility that the people creating the documents may be unrepresentative. Although there are many social research data sources, five broad types are summarized below, for context.

- **Interviews:** The researcher identifies a sample of people relative to the research question, interviews them in person or remotely and analyzes the transcripts of the interviews using a text analysis method, such as thematic analysis (Braun and Clarke, 2006, 2013) or content analysis (Neuendorf, 2016).

- **Surveys:** The researcher designs a questionnaire with closed questions and (often) some open questions and then (usually) sends it to a large set (hundreds or thousands) of people in the target group. Closed questions can be analyzed with descriptive or inferential statistics. Open questions may be analyzed informally or with a text analysis method, such as content analysis or thematic analysis.

- **Statistical data:** The researcher obtains data about the target population from existing sources and analyzes them statistically to obtain conclusions about the relationships between variables. For example, the relationship between poverty and academic achievement might be analyzed with national government statistics about school performance, combined with a different set of national government data about poverty levels in the catchment areas of each school.

- **Social web texts:** The researcher gathers a set of topic-relevant texts from a social website, such as based on a set of queries and analyzes them with a text analysis method.

- **Documents:** The researcher obtains a sample or complete set of documents encapsulating the issue to be discussed and then analyzes them with a text analysis or discourse analysis method. This is common in corpus linguistics to identify patterns of language use from sets of novels, genres, or natural language transcripts. It is also used in the scientometrics field to analyze patterns of scientific investigation from the titles and/or abstracts of journal articles.

This book describes word association analysis methods to analyze texts from social websites or other document collections: the last two in the above list.

While the information from closed survey questions can be analyzed with statistics, qualitative methods, such as thematic analysis, discourse analysis, or content analysis, are needed to explore the text produced by open-ended survey questions, interviews and focus groups. All research methods have limitations (Table 1.3), with the nature of these limitations varying between methods. These methods are time consuming (for the investigator; also needing participant time), require ethical approval (also takes time), and the ability to generalize may be limited by small samples (interviews, focus groups) or unrepresentative samples (e.g., self-selection or sampling biases for most surveys).

Table 1.3: A comparison of factors affecting a selection of text-based social research data

Factor	Interviews	Surveys	Statistical	Social web	Documents
Time	Labor intensive to organize and conduct	Labor intensive to design and sample well	Labor intensive to learn	Labor intensive to learn	Labor intensive to learn
Sample Bias	Small, impossible to be representative	Selection and self-selection biases common	Depends on sources	Social web user bias	Depends on sources
Ethics	Approval and safeguards needed	Approval needed	Approval often not needed	Approval often not needed if public	Approval not needed if public
IT	Recommended (e.g., Nvivo)	Statistical software	Statistical software	Specialist software	Specialist software
Topic Bias	Researcher questions and participant suggestions	Researcher questions and participant suggestions	Researcher ideas	Participant topics of interest	Scope of document collections

1.5 SOFTWARE: MOZDEH

This book draws upon methods implemented within the free Windows software Mozdeh (http://mozdeh.wlv.ac.uk). Researchers without access to a Windows computer (or a computer with Windows as part of a dual installation, such as through Boot Camp on a Mac) will need to borrow one for the first stage of the method.

Mozdeh can harvest data from selected social network sites (Twitter and YouTube at the time of writing) and save it to the local computer for processing. It can also import texts from other sources. Its analysis interface has buttons for all the word association analyses described in this book. Conducting any type of word association analysis with Mozdeh therefore entails collecting/importing and processing with the software, but the investigator still needs to interpret the Mozdeh outputs.

1.6 LANGUAGE AND INTERNATIONAL CONSIDERATIONS

The methods described in this book apply, in theory, to any written language on the Internet, although the examples below are all for English-language texts. The start of the WATA method involves comparing the frequency of words across sets of text in the same language, which can be any single language. There is one caveat, however. Some written languages (e.g., Burmese, Chinese, Japanese, Khmer, Lao, Thai, and Vietnamese) do not use spaces or other markers between words, leaving the reader to group characters into words to understand the meaning of a text. This causes a problem for the methods in this book that work at the level of words. There are algorithms that can split texts into words for the above languages, however. The above-mentioned software Mozdeh incorporates a word segmenting-tool of this kind for Japanese (atilika, 2014), but for other languages an external program would be needed (e.g., Manning et al., 2014), with the output fed into Mozdeh.

Many languages are extensively spoken in multiple countries and many countries have substantial numbers of native speakers of multiple languages. Since the methods in this book work within a single language, consideration must be given to (a) which language to focus on, (b) how to ensure that only people from the desired country or countries are included for that language, and (c) whether to run multiple studies, one per language, if there are multiple important languages. For example, a study of social media use in the U.S. might want to collect tweets in both English and Spanish for two parallel studies and consider how to ensure that the tweet authors largely exclude English and Spanish speakers from elsewhere in the world (Mozdeh can help with this for tweets but not for YouTube comments).

1.7 USING THIS BOOK

This book describes the core word association analysis and word association thematic analysis methods, outlining how to conduct them with Mozdeh, explaining the rationale behind the methods used and relevant considerations for researchers. It is important to try out the methods a few times before starting a full-scale research project so that key early decisions (particularly for data collection) do not lead to invalid research projects. It is therefore essential to experiment with the methods after each chapter. Pilot datasets for this should be as large as possible because the methods are more powerful and insightful for larger collections of texts, so a small sample is likely to give disappointing results.

The book is arranged in a linear sequence, where many chapters depend on previous chapters. It is therefore best read in sequential order except that some chapters can be skipped.

- **Data collection with Mozdeh:** Skip the subsections not relevant to your project.

- **Word association detection statistical details:** This can be skipped if you are not interested in the statistical background to the methods.
- **Word association thematic analysis chapters:** These can be omitted if you expect a small sample of texts or otherwise do not need a thematic analysis.
- **Comparison with other methods:** This can be safely skipped but this information may be useful when justifying your research methods in your dissertation, thesis, or article.

CHAPTER 2

Data Collection with Mozdeh

This chapter gives a brief overview of the generic issues involved with collecting data, together with examples for Twitter and YouTube and an overview of the Mozdeh procedures. It finishes with a discussion about importing texts, with the example of academic publication metadata.

2.1 SAMPLE SIZE

For all sources of texts, a large sample is needed for a reasonable analysis. This is because there are unlikely to be statistically significant differences in small sets of texts. If a reference set of texts is being used, then the guideline can be halved because the reference set adds to the statistical power of the initial word frequency test. As a rough guideline, the following minimum numbers of texts are recommended.

- 10,000 is the minimum for any kind of analysis, or 5,000 if there is also a larger reference set. This will only be enough if they are tightly focused on a topic. More will be needed for loose topics where the texts cover many issues.
- 100,000 is the recommended minimum number of texts to analyze in normal circumstances, or 50,000 if there is also a larger reference set. If this is not possible then another analysis approach may be preferable.

2.2 DATA COLLECTION METHODS

2.2.1 QUERY-BASED POST COLLECTION (TWITTER)

A common way to start a social media analysis project with Mozdeh or any other analytics tool is to build a set of queries to match the topic investigated. In the easiest case, the query might be defined by the project itself. For example, an analysis of a Twitter campaign based around one or more hashtags would use those hashtags as the queries (Makita et al., 2020; Potts and Radford, 2019). In this case, the decision to use the hashtags is straightforward if most tweets within the campaign are expected to use them. A distinctive and almost unique word may also be a suitable query if it is reasonable to expect most relevant tweets to contain it. For example, the single query BRCA has been used to focus on the cancer community around the BRCA gene mutation (Vicari, 2020), variants of the name *Intizar* for a study of reactions in Turkey to her outing as LGBTQI+

(Ozduzen and Korkut, 2020), different names for Boko Haram for a study of reactions to the organization in Nigeria (Ette and Joe, 2018), and the phrase query "climate change" has been used for a broad focus (Holmberg and Hellsten, 2015). In other situations, considerable time may be needed to curate an appropriate set of queries. To illustrate this, one issue was tracked on Twitter with many different keywords and hashtags (Ahmed et al., 2018). The rest of this subsection deals with this issue. Although query-based data collection is possible with YouTube and supported by Mozdeh, it is usually less effective than user-based data collection, so this section focuses on Twitter. The suggestions here can also be modified for other contexts where queries are used to collect a set of texts for word association analyses.

The usual solution to the need for query-based data collection is a set of queries, each of which matches the topic in a different way. For example, for the topic of tennis, the queries might be the word "tennis" and the names of current famous tennis players. The most important point is that each query must not generate many false matches. Ideally, each query should generate less than 10% false matches. This is important because the word association tests do not work well if the data collected includes a large share of irrelevant texts. This should be evaluated by submitting the query to twitter.com and estimating the proportion of relevant matches from the matching tweets that it shows.

The jargon word relevant here is "precision," which means the percentage of search matches that match our intended topic. For example, if a search for "Coco Gauff" should give 100% "precision": all of the tweets would be about the tennis player with this name because it is relatively rare. In contrast, searches for emerging tennis star "Sarah Smith" might find a precision of 50%: only 50% of the tweets matching this phrase might be about the tennis player because she has a common name. Many of the matching tweets might be about other Sarah Smiths.

There are two goals for curating a set of appropriate queries: (a) avoid too many false matches and (b) get as many correct matches as possible. This usually entails spending up to a week testing candidate queries to build up a large high-precision query collection. The golden rule is test, test, test: don't assume that a query will generate mainly relevant results without testing it thoroughly first. Time spent creating a good set of queries will be repaid with high quality data at a later stage.

To generate candidate queries, the main technique is to think about the different aspects of the topic that people might tweet about and the words that they might use to do so. Considering the topic of tennis, people might use the term itself or might discuss its equipment (racket, ball, net, court), scores (love-30), or players. The equipment queries are likely to be low precision because of other sports using equipment with the same name, but a lot of famous tennis players are likely to have names that produce high precision queries on Twitter, and the same might be true for some tennis scores—testing is needed to check. In summary:

1. brainstorm a list of aspects of the topic that might be tweeted about;

2. deduce a list of words or phrases that might be used in tweets about each aspect of the topic;

3. test the words and phrases at twitter.com and reject those with more than 10% irrelevant matches; and

4. enter the final list of query words and phrases into Mozdeh.

The choice of queries used will influence the results of a project and so the choice must be justified, and any limitations acknowledged. For example, a project investigating tweets about COVID-19 used the following four queries: coronavirus; "corona virus"; COVID-19; and COVID19 (Thelwall and Thelwall, 2020). These are all relatively high precision queries (even the first two, which could be referring to other coronaviruses), but do not capture tweets about COVID-19 that do not mention it by name. This is an important limitation that the paper should have mentioned.

2.2.2 USER-BASED POST COLLECTION (TWITTER, YOUTUBE)

In contrast to query-based data collection, user-based data collection entails specifying the texts to be collected in terms of the people that created them (Twitter) or the people/channels that created the videos that the comments are attached to (YouTube). This is relevant to projects that naturally focus on one person or a set of people that are identified in advance by their role offline (e.g., politicians) or on social media (e.g., Tweeters related to the Filter Wales anti-smoking organization; van Diepen, 2018).

On Twitter, it is straightforward to collect the tweets by a set of users from a list of their Twitter @usernames. On YouTube it is impossible to gather all comments by individual users because comments can only be extracted from video pages. Thus, to collect YouTube comments, the first stage is to specify the videos that are to be checked for comments. This can be done in three ways.

- **Video URLs:** A list of these can be manually created through any systematic method, such as querying YouTube.com and selecting relevant videos.

- **Channel URLs:** All videos are part of the YouTube channel of the person that uploaded them. Videos can be specified by channel (i.e., uploader) rather than individually. For this, any systematic method can be used to manually identify one or more relevant YouTube channel URLs.

- **Query terms:** Specifying a query to match videos is not recommended because video titles can be highly varied and not good indicators of the content of a video.

2.2.3 USER PROFILE BIO COLLECTION (TWITTER)

Each Twitter user can enter a short profile description to appear near the top of their Twitter homepage, although about a third of users enter nothing. Sometimes key information about the user is contained in this text, such their nonbinary gender, job, hobbies, or political affiliations. A project could analyze these profile descriptions rather than people's tweets to investigate what they say about themselves rather than what they comment on. There is no list of all tweeters so a project investigating Twitter bios would need to identify tweeters by another method, such as obtaining a set of tweets with appropriate queries and then downloading the bios of the corresponding tweeters (Mozdeh can list them).

2.2.4 OTHER METHODS TO IDENTIFY A SET OF TEXTS FOR ANALYSIS

There are many other methods to obtain a set of texts for analysis. In particular, a project might have access to a complete set of texts from a given source and analyze them all or select relevant texts through any metadata. For example, a WATA for academic documents had access to a complete set and selected the analysis set by first author geographic affiliation (Thelwall, et al., 2019a).

2.3 MOZDEH DATA COLLECTION PROCEDURES

This section gives an overview of the main considerations when collecting or importing texts with the free software Mozdeh (http://mozdeh.wlv.ac.uk) used in this book. Detailed instructions about how to use the program are on its website. At the time of writing, Mozdeh can collect tweets or YouTube comments directly or import sets of texts from other sources. Mozdeh can collect and process texts in any language but, as mentioned in the Introduction, there are special considerations for written languages that do not use spaces between words. Mozdeh has been used for Korean (Kim, 2020), Russian (Chernyaev et al., 2020), and Turkish (Ozduzen and McGarry, 2020), for example.

For a little background context, when Mozdeh is downloaded and started, it creates a folder called *moz_data* on the local computer to store the texts it collects. When starting a new project, it creates a subfolder and stores all the texts in that subfolder. The results of analyses performed on the texts are stored in a subfolder of the project folder called *reports* (Figure 2.1). All the other subfolders of the project folder can be safely ignored, unless the original texts are needed for any purpose: they are stored in the *raw data* folder.

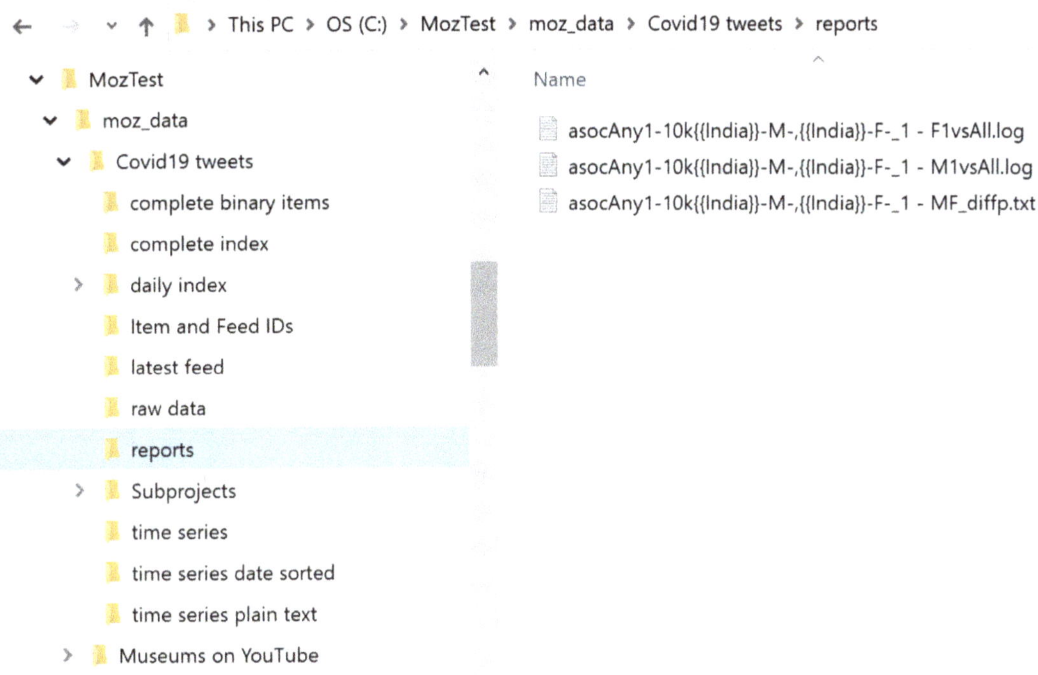

Figure 2.1: The moz_data folder structure created by Mozdeh, showing two project folders (Covid19 tweets and Museums on YouTube) and three text files in the Reports folder (right-hand side) after running a Male v. Female gender comparison of Indian tweets.

2.3.1 QUERY-BASED POST COLLECTION IN MOZDEH

Once a set of queries has been designed, they can be entered into Mozdeh. It will submit them to Twitter and retrieve matching tweets until you tell it to stop. Figure 2.2 shows Mozdeh after being left collecting English-language Covid-19 tweets for 13 days. The title bar shows that it has collected over 9 million tweets in this time (and that it has checked Twitter for new tweets 155,908 times). The queries shown were all selected for being high precision (very specific to Covid-19 in early 2020) even though only one mentions the virus name.

A frustrating limitation when collecting tweets with Mozdeh with queries is that it cannot collect tweets that are older than ten days, and in any case can only access the most recent about 5,000 tweets matching a query (these are Twitter limitations). In practice, Mozdeh might even not be able to retrieve tweets older than 1 hour for popular topics because of the 5,000 limitation. A less critical problem is that Mozdeh does not return all matching tweets because Twitter does not share them all. This seems to affect queries generating many results per day (e.g., 100,000 daily tweets) much more than queries with fewer results (Thelwall, 2015). As this book was about to go to press in January 2021, Twitter announced that it would share older tweets free with researchers through its Academic Research offering (https://developer.twitter.com/en/solutions/academic-research). The default ten day tweet age limitation may therefore be lifted for academics and students approved by Twitter.

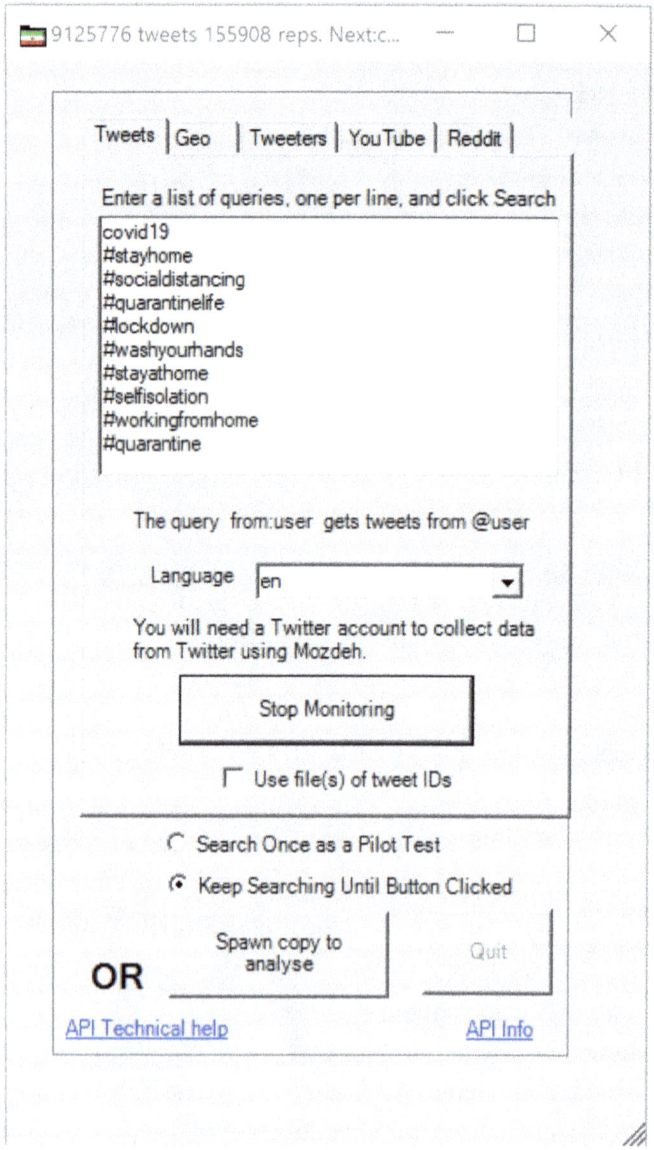

Figure 2.2: The Mozdeh data collection interface for Twitter after 13 days collecting tweets with 10 queries. The *Keep Searching Until Button Clicked* option is checked, telling Mozdeh to keep going until told to stop.

For tweets collected based on a set of queries in this way, a maximum of one tweet should be allowed per user or the results may be dominated by the preoccupations of individual prolific tweeters. After stopping the data collection, Mozdeh asks a series of questions about how to process the data: it is important to select the option to include a maximum of one tweet per user.

2.3.2 USER-BASED POST COLLECTION WITH MOZDEH

Mozdeh collects recent tweets from a set of users by entering their Twitter usernames in the Tweeters tab of the data collection screen. It collects comments on YouTube videos by either entering a list of video URLs or YouTube user channel URLs into the YouTube tab of the data collection screen (see Figure 2.2).

2.3.3 USER PROFILE BIO COLLECTION WITH MOZDEH

Mozdeh can download Twitter profile bios, but first a list of usernames is needed. Usernames can be identified indirectly by searching for tweets and then downloading the profiles of the authors of these tweets. For example, if a set of tweets about Covid-19 was collected then the profiles of the tweeters could be downloaded (Thelwall et al., submitted). This is therefore a two-stage process. After collecting tweets using a relevant set of queries and opening the main Mozdeh search screen with these tweets, the profiles can be downloaded by Mozdeh using its Advanced menu option "Report user descriptions when clicking on results." The primary purpose of this is to show user profile information alongside the users' tweets in Mozdeh. As a side-effect, Mozdeh saves the user profile descriptions in a file called *UserInfoFile.txt* in the *moz_data* folder it creates to contain its projects. To load these profile descriptions into Mozdeh, start a new Mozdeh project, click the Import Data button, select the Twitter data type, select the UserInfoFile.txt in the *moz_data* folder and click the Users button in the *Mozdeh Conversion Options* window. This creates a new Mozdeh project with Twitter user profile descriptions.

2.3.4 IMPORTING TEXT COLLECTIONS (ACADEMIC PUBLICATIONS, OTHER) INTO MOZDEH

Mozdeh can import text data from any source if it is first saved to a plain text file, with one text per line. Mozdeh can perform richer word association tests if the text file also contains other information, such as usernames (allowing gender-based word association analyses), post dates (allowing time-based WAA), and post scores (e.g., retweets or citations, allowing score-based WAA). If this extra information is included, then the text file must be in tab-delimited format (with the additional information entered on each line after a tab). A simple way to get this information into tab-delimited form is to copy it into a spreadsheet, with the text in one column and the other information in separate columns, then using the spreadsheet option to save the worksheet in Windows tab-delimited format.

Mozdeh can read a pre-defined set of tab-delimited formats. These include academic metadata from the Scopus database, for example. Files saved by Scopus in tab-delimited (Windows) format can be read into Mozdeh, where it will recognize the names of the authors, the citation counts (as scores) and the publication date. The Import Data button in Mozdeh gives a list of the currently supported sources (Figure 2.3).

Although Mozdeh only collects texts from Twitter and YouTube, methods exist to capture text from Instagram (Scherr et al., 2020) and other sites. If these are converted into a simple plain text or tab-delimited format then they could be read into Mozdeh.

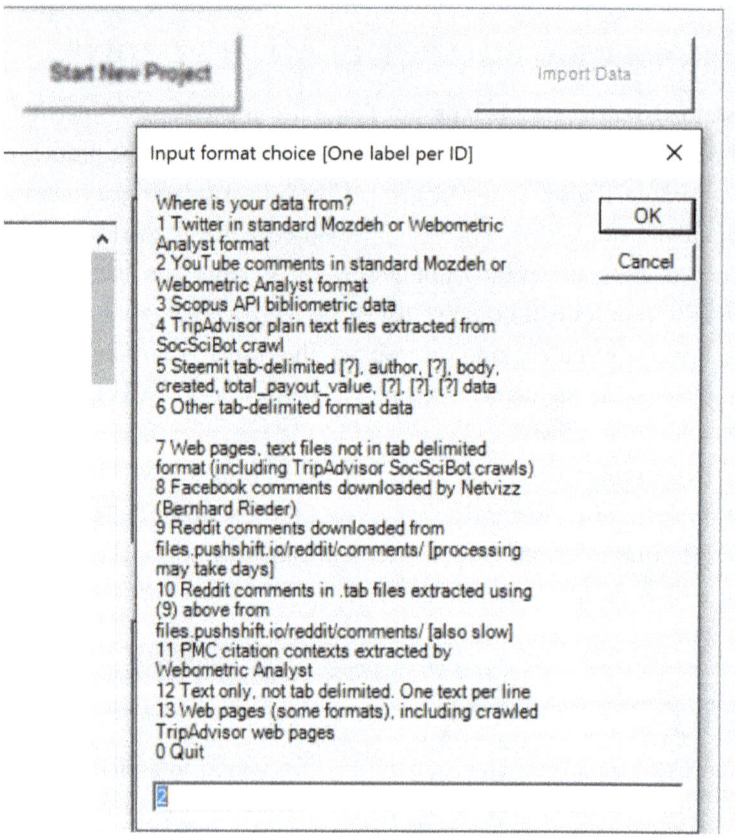

Figure 2.3: Mozdeh after starting it, entering a new project name, and clicking on the Import Data button (top right). The Input format choice dialog box lists the 13 different formats that it recognizes. Two are generic: 6 (any tab delimited format) and 12 (text only).

2.4 FILTERING THE INITIAL DATASET

The data collection process might retrieve some texts that are not relevant for the analysis. For example, a study of Brexit might want to focus on UK tweeters, but it is not possible to specify the UK only when collecting tweets (geolocated queries do not work well). Similarly, a project might want to focus on female YouTube commenters, whereas gender cannot be specified when downloading comments. In cases like these, Mozdeh can create a copy of a project with only the texts matching a query or filters (e.g., UK location, female gender). This option is in the Save tab of the main search screen.

2.5 SUMMARY

The set of texts to be analyzed can, at the time of writing, be collected from Twitter through queries, from Twitter by specifying a list of users or from YouTube by specifying a list of videos or channels. It can also be imported from other sources. It is important to ensure that the text collection is high quality for processing, in the sense of containing few irrelevant or spam texts, or the word association analysis methods will not work well. If using the Twitter query method, the data collection must be planned carefully because Twitter does not share tweets free that are older than a week, and for popular topics, only tweets from the hour of data collection might be collected. Step-by-step instructions for these tasks are on the Mozdeh website.

CHAPTER 3

Word Association Detection: Term Identification

Word association analysis (WAA) is a method to find words that are more prevalent in one set of texts than another, detecting their meaning and context. For the first part, word association detection (WAD), Mozdeh detects words that are relatively more common in one set of texts than another. The second part (word association contextualization; see Chapter 4) identifies their meaning and context. More specifically, WAD is a method to find words that are:

1. in a higher percentage of texts in subset A than in subset B, where
2. the difference between the two percentages is statistically significant.

Suppose that in a collection of Covid-19 tweets, subset A contains Covid-19 tweets by males and subset B contains Covid-19 tweets by females (Table 3.1). If the word "nurse" occurred in 60% of the tweets in set A but 40% of the tweets in set B then it would satisfy condition 1 above but a statistical test would be needed for condition 2 to check if the difference between 40% and 60% was statistically significant. Statistical significance tests are conducted automatically by Mozdeh and this chapter gives information to understand the results. Statistical tests are important because small percentage differences can easily occur by accident.

Table 3.1: Ten tweets where 60% of the female-authored tweets and 40% of the male-authored tweets contain "nurse"

Male-Authored Tweets (subset A)	Female-Authored Tweets (subset B)
I appreciated that *nurse*.	I am a *nurse* and am tired today.
I clapped for the *nurse* that saved me.	I feel sorry for the *nurse* on duty today.
The doctors helped a lot.	An NHS *nurse* from Zimbabwe died today.
I want to go out and play footy.	I never have time to sit down.
The politicians got it badly wrong.	Did a shopping run for my parents today.

The result of a word association analysis is a list of words that occur in a statistically significantly higher percentage of tweets in one subset than another. For example, if the two subsets are Covid-19 tweets by males and females then this would give two lists of words: those that are in a higher percentage of female-authored tweets (e.g., "nurse" in the example above) and those that are in a higher percentage of male-authored tweets, together with evidence of statistical significance (in the form of stars, as explained below).

3.1 WORD ASSOCIATION DETECTION: SUBSET VS. THE REST

There are two types of WAD test. The first, subset vs. the rest, extracts words that occur in a higher proportion of texts in the specified subset than in the remaining texts (Figure 3.1). The second, subset A vs. subset B, compares words between two subsets, ignoring the remainder (Figure 3.2). To illustrate the first case, one study has collected tweets about 100 diseases, disorders, and medical contexts. For the subset of tweets mentioning ADHD, a subset vs. the rest test would identify terms that are in a higher percentage of ADHD tweets than tweets about the other conditions (Thelwall et al., 2021). To illustrate this, if the word "fidgeting" was mentioned in 50% of the ADHD tweets and 20% of the rest then it would be detected as associating with ADHD (Table 3.2).

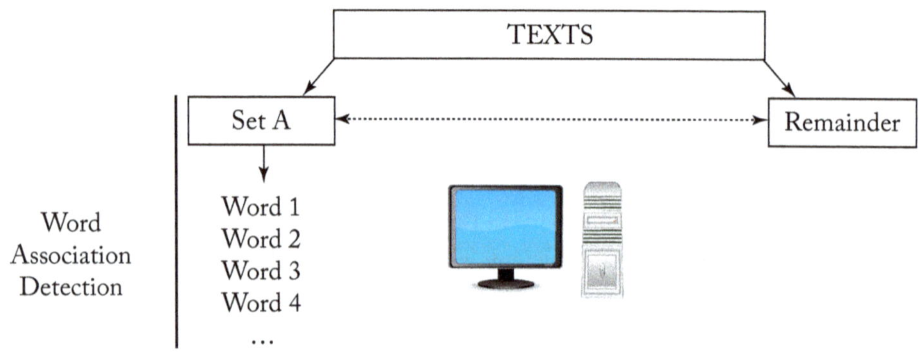

Figure 3.1: Word association detection for a subset of the texts analyzed against the remaining texts.

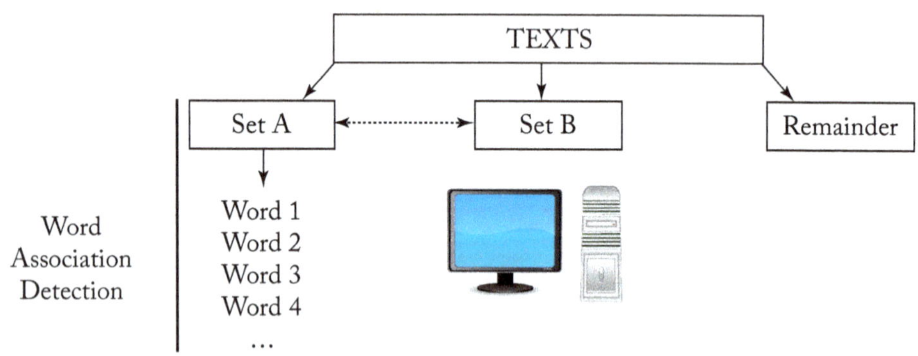

Figure 3.2: Word association detection for subset A of the texts analyzed against another subset.

Table 3.2: An example set of tweets for a subset vs. the rest test in the case of ADHD

ADHD (subset)	Not ADHD (the rest)
My ADHD is flaring.	I am fidgeting trying not to scratch.
I was diagnosed with ADHD.	Doc said I have depression.
I am fidgeting with my ADHD.	They are testing me for bipolar.
Have been fidgeting all day from ADHD.	The operation scar was agony.
	I got to see the lead singer for my Wish.

Word association detection is too time-consuming for a human to carry out except on tiny numbers of texts. In the above example, it is possible to individually check all the words in the ADHD subset of Table 3.2 to find out which terms are more common in this set than the other. These words are: ADHD (4 out of 4 or 100% in the ADHD subset A compared to 0 out of 5 or 0% of the rest); my (50% vs. 0%); is (25% vs. 0%); flaring (25% vs. 0%); was (25% vs. 20%); diagnosed (25% vs. 0%); with (50% vs. 0%); fidgeting (50% vs. 20%); am (25% vs. 20%); have (25% vs. 20%); been (25% vs. 0%); all (25% vs. 0%); day (25% vs. 0%); from (25% vs. 0%). In contrast, the only word that occurs in the ADHD subset but does not form a higher percentage than in the rest is: I (50% vs. 60%). Thus, for Table 3.2, the WAD test results would be the words that have occur in a higher percentage of tweets in the ADHD subset: ADHD, my, is, flaring, was, diagnosed, with, fidgeting, am, have, been, all, day, from. This is not a very useful list, but lists produced from much larger sets of texts tend to be far more informative because they reflect general trends rather than individual tweets.

3.1.1 CHOICE OF COMPARATOR SET

The remainder comparator set (i.e., "the rest" in the subset vs. the rest) must be comparable as possible to the subset analyzed for the WAD stage to work well. This is because WATA will focus on differences between the subset and the remaining tweets, and any mismatches may appear as irrelevant topics in the results. Here are some examples of problematic remainder sets, and suggested solutions.

People subset vs. mixed human/organizational remainder. A study collects tweets mentioning ADHD and applied WAD to the subset of tweets from people apparently with ADHD. In this case, the remaining tweets (i.e., tweets mentioning ADHD but not from people with ADHD) is not the best comparator set because it will contain organizational Twitter accounts, such as from schools and ADHD support organizations. Thus, textual differences between tweets from people with ADHD and the remainder might include words like "breakfast," "omg," and "mates" that are more likely to be used by human tweeters than organizational tweeters and are irrelevant to ADHD. A simple way to largely avoid this is to exclude tweets from people that do not have a recognized human first name, so that the comparator set is (largely) from human tweeters (in Mozdeh, this can be achieved by applying a male or female or nonbinary gender filter to exclude accounts without a recognized gender).

Country focused subset vs. international remainder. A study collects English-language tweets mentioning COVID-19 and analyzes the subset mentioning contemporary Prime Minister Boris Johnson. This would be problematic because the remainder would include many non-UK tweets so the WAD word found would partly reflect Boris Johnson and partly reflect UK-international differences. This issue can be resolved by excluding all non-UK tweets so that the remainder set is also UK-based.

It is useful to browse some tweets from the remainder set for a project to check that it is not incompatible with the subset analyzed. If problems are found, then it may be possible to devise a strategy to make the remainder set more comparable, as in the cases of the people and country-focused subsets above.

3.1.2 WORD ASSOCIATION DETECTION WITH MOZDEH

In practice, word association detection needs a computer program, such as Mozdeh to automate. Mozdeh can quickly check each word in the subset to see if it occurs in a higher percentage of subset tweets than tweets from the rest, saving a huge amount of time.

The comparisons can be more powerful if singular and plural words are combined for the purpose of counting, since their meanings are almost identical. When Mozdeh conducts word association detection, it automatically combines singular and plural words. In Table 3.3, the word "hug" occurs in 25% (1 out of 4) after lockdown tweets and 25% (2 out of 8) during lockdown tweets and the word "hugs" occurs in 50% (2 out of 4) after lockdown tweets and 0% of during lockdown tweets (Table 3.3). Mozdeh would not report any of these but would instead report that hug(s) occurs in 75% of after lockdown tweets and 25% of during lockdown tweets. This is simpler and more useful information. Note that Mozdeh works by (basic) depluralization: automatically chopping the final "s" from words. It reports only the singular version of the word in its output list.

Table 3.3: An example set of tweets for a subset (after lockdown) vs. the rest (during lockdown) test in the case of Covid-19

After Lockdown Tweets (subset)	During Lockdown Tweets (the rest)
I got lots of hugs from everyone!!!	Wish I could hug someone.
My favorite hug was with by bf.	Am very scared of shopping.
Still waiting for hugs with gran.	Worried about getting a job at the end.
The COVID-19 antibody test was positive.	In lockdown with my bf, not so bad.😊
	We clapped for key workers, now pay them!
	I can't hug my family until after quarantine.
	Winston skypes grandad daily.
	The doctor rang to say she'd died overnight.

The subset for WAD can be defined in Mozdeh by a query, filters (sentiment, gender, retweets, or other score) or a combination of both. For example, the subset might consist of all tweets expressing a positive sentiment. In this case the WAD results would include words that express positive sentiment, and things that people are positive about. WAD applied to positive tweets against the rest from a collection of tweets from tweeters with disabilities might find sentiment words like "love" and other words like "zoom" (Table 3.4) to occur in a higher percentage of positive tweets (50% vs. 0% or 20%).

Table 3.4: An example set of tweets for a subset (positive sentiment) vs. the rest (not positive sentiment) test in the case of tweeters with disabilities during Covid-19

Positive Tweets (subset)	Not Positive (the rest)
I love zoom, easy peasy!	Scared of getting covid from my carers.
A food delivery at last, wowwww!!!	Have to fend for myself now, can't risk it.
Love working from home—no travel.	Another day another Weetabix.
Zoom is great, am well used to it.	Might go on tiktok or zoom.
	We are being super careful to avoid covid.

The main Mozdeh filters are as follows (Figure 3.3).

- **Sentiment:** The subset is defined by its positive or negative sentiment strength. For example, it might be all tweets expressing moderate or strong negative sentiment, as estimated by the inbuilt sentiment analysis software SentiStrength (Thelwall, Buckley, and Paltoglou, 2012).

- **Gender:** The subset is defined by the gender of the user. For example, it might be all tweets where the tweeter appears to be female (i.e., their username seems to start with a female first name). Only male and female are supported for YouTube comments and imported data since other genders to not commonly have distinctive first names. For Twitter, Mozdeh can also detect nonbinary genders (as a single group) for users that list they/them pronouns in their profiles.

- **Country (Tweets or Imported data only):** The subset is defined by a single country. To activate this for Twitter in Mozdeh, select "Get countries of Twitter users" from the Advanced menu, after loading a project.
- **Time:** Date ranges can be specified in Mozdeh by adding the number of the first and last data in square brackets after a query (e.g., "hat [3 5]" would match all texts containing the word hat and posted between the third and fifth date in the data).
- **Retweets (or other score):** The subset is the set of tweets (or texts) that have at least a minimum (or at most a maximum) retweet count (or other score).

All these filters are imperfect, and researchers should check that they are accurate enough for their purposes, reporting their limitations if they impinge on a study. The sentiment scores are approximate using the SentiStrength lexical algorithm (Thelwall, Buckley, and Paltoglou, 2012) that looks for sentiment-related terms or phrases and can be fooled by polysemy, sarcasm, figurative language, and indirectness. The gender detection is based on common first names, discarding people with first names that are rare in the host country, such as people using pseudonyms, and people with ethnic or cultural minority names, gender-neutral nicknames (e.g., Alex) and from gender-neutral naming cultures (e.g., Sikh). Country location information from Twitter in Mozdeh excludes people not from large cities that do not declare their country. Time in Mozdeh is also slightly ambiguous since days start at different times globally. Retweet counts can be incorrect if multiple copies of a tweet are retweeted or if a tweet continued to be retweeted after the version collected by Mozdeh. In each case, accuracy can be checked in Mozdeh with a random sample of texts and the results of the test reported, together with a judgement about whether the accuracy is sufficient for the research purposes.

A subset vs. the rest test can be run in Mozdeh by entering a query or filter in the main search screen, then clicking the "Mine associations for search and filters" button (Figure 3.4). A list of terms that occur in a higher proportion of texts in the subset than in the remaining texts will appear on screen in the bottom right hand corner. These results can be copied to a file to save them.

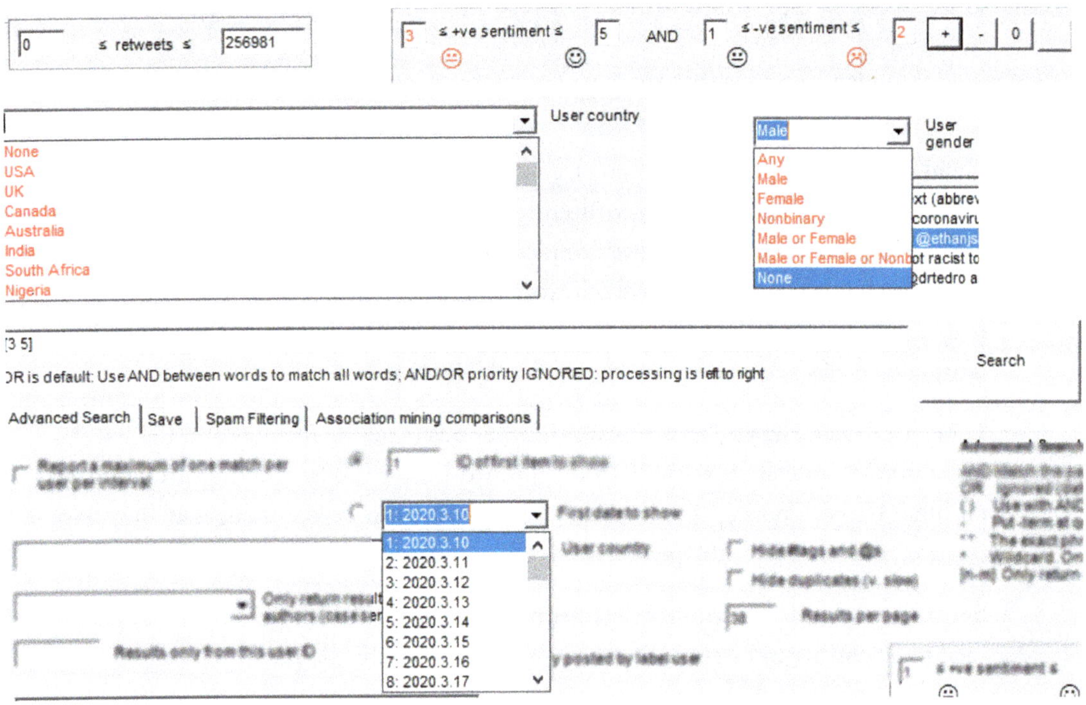

Figure 3.3: Filter options available in the Mozdeh search screen: retweets/score (left); sentiment (top right); country (middle left); gender (middle right); and date (bottom, showing the date range [3 5] in the search box and the drop-down box with dates indicating that 3 is 2020.3.12 and 5 is 2020.3.14).

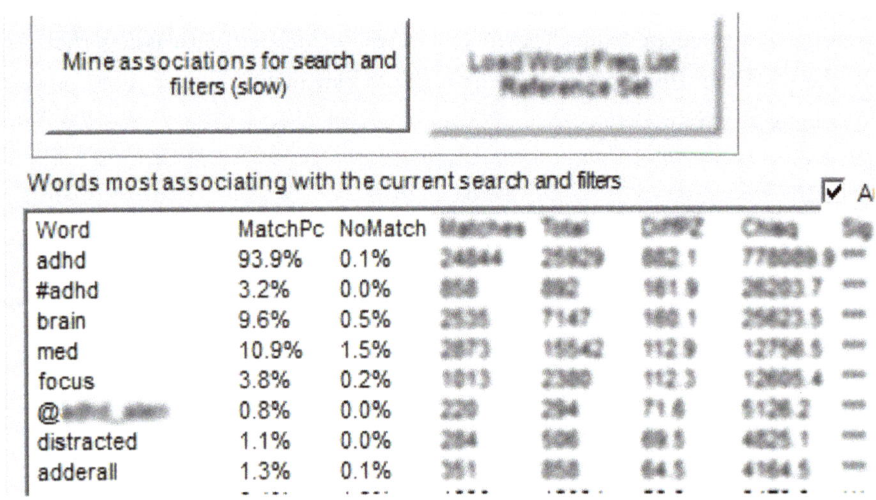

Figure 3.4: Mozdeh after selecting an ADHD filter and clicking the *Mine associations for search and filters* button. The fourth row indicates that the term "brain" occurs in 9.6% of the ADHD tweets and 0.5% of the rest. Stars in the final column indicate statistically significant differences.

3.2 WORD ASSOCIATION DETECTION: SUBSET A VS. SUBSET B

It can be useful to identify words that are more common in one subset than another within a larger set of texts. Here are some examples (see Figure 3.5).

- **Gender:** To detect gender differences, compare texts written by females against those written by males, ignoring texts written by people with other genders, bots, organizations or people with names that do not reveal their genders. A WAD would reveal words used in a higher percentage of texts authored by females than texts authored by males, and vice versa. Texts written by nonbinary users can be compared against texts written by males and females combined for the same reason.

- **Date:** To detect changes between two time periods (e.g., the first day and the last day of an event), compare texts written on the two time periods, ignoring texts written on other dates. Ignoring intermediate dates can help to detect changes if they have occurred gradually over the period analyzed.

- **Sentiment:** Comparing positive against negative texts can identify things that people tend to be positive or negative about, ignoring the texts that do not express an opinion.

- **Topics:** Comparing texts in one topic (e.g., as specified by a keyword query) against another can be especially useful to detect differences between two otherwise similar topics, such as two related diseases or disorders.

- **Retweets or scores:** Comparing texts with a high score against texts with a low score, ignoring intermediate values, can detect words associated with issues that resonate on the platform. Ignoring intermediate values can make the test more powerful by focusing on extreme cases.

Subset	Remaining Tweets
Tweets including "ADHD"	Tweets not including "ADHD"
Positive tweets	Tweets that are not positive
Tweets from Day 1	Tweets from any other day
Tweets with 10+ retweets	Tweets with 0–9 retweets

Subset A	Subset B	Remaining Tweets
Female-authored tweets	Male-authored tweets	Tweets not by males or females
Tweets from Week 1	Tweets from Week 26	Tweets from Weeks 2–25
Positive tweets	Negative tweets	Neutral or mixed tweets
Tweets about bipolar	Tweets about depression	Tweets about other conditions
Tweets with 100+ retweets	Tweets with 0 retweets	Tweets with 1–99 retweets

Figure 3.5: The two types of Word Association Analysis: Subset vs. the rest (top) and subset A vs. subset B (bottom), with multiple examples of each. In the bottom cases the remaining tweets are ignored, but in the top cases they are included (red vs. blue in all cases).

To illustrate the subset A vs. subset B test, suppose that tweets have been during and after the WOMAD world music, arts and dance festival. In order to assess whether people had found new things to enjoy, someone might look for things mentioned in tweets afterwards that had not been mentioned before (Table 3.5). A word association test for subset A against subset B in this tiny made-up case would find the terms "Angelique" and "Kidjo" (among others) since they occurred in 50% of after tweets and 0% of before tweets. In contrast, the words "Flaming" and "lips" occurred in 50% before and 50% after (from The Flaming Lips band name) so they would not be detected. Of the two acts, Angelique Kidjo was the unexpected success.

Table 3.5: An example set of tweets for a subset A (tweets before WOMAD) vs. subset B (tweets after WOMAD) ignoring the remainder (tweets during WOMAD)

Day	Tweets
Day before WOMAD	Looking forward to meeting friends! Hope to see Flaming Lips.
WOMAD day 1	Angelique Kidjo was amazing!!!! Too busy dancing to tweet, sorry mum x
WOMAD day 2	Danced all day at the open air stage.
WOMAD day 2	Kids had fun at the World of Wellbeing.
Day after WOMAD	Angelique Kidjo was the best – am a fan now! Flaming Lips did not disappoint.

Subset A vs. subset A tests can be run in Mozdeh using the options in the "Association mining comparisons" tab in the main search screen. After this, two search terms to be compared can be entered the in the text box in the middle of this tab, with a comma in the middle. For example, to run word association tests that compare bipolar disorder tweets to tweets about depression, enter "bipolar, depression" in this box, then clicking the "Compare words matching the above queries…" button (Figure 3.6). A list of terms that occur in a higher percentage of texts in subset A than in subset B, or the other way around, will be found and saved to a file with name ending in "_diffp". This can be opened in a spreadsheet to read (Figure 3.7).

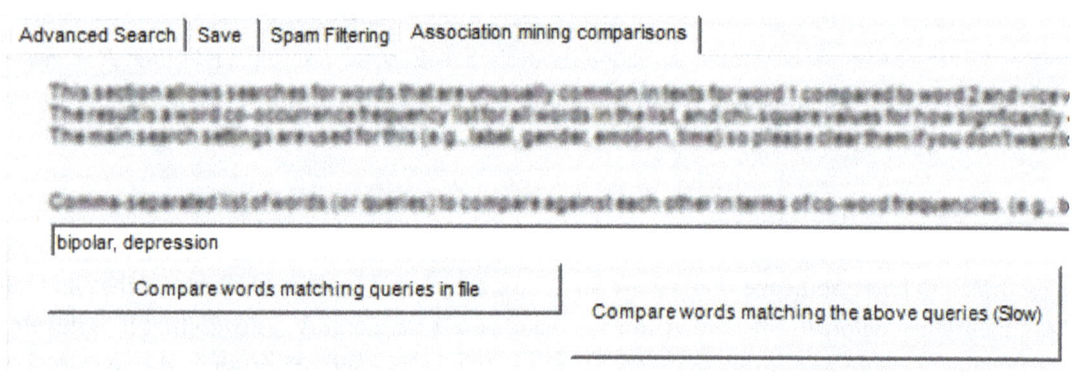

Figure 3.6: The Mozdeh *Association mining comparisons* tab with the queries bipolar and depression entered to be compared—the bottom right button will conduct a WAD on texts matching these two terms.

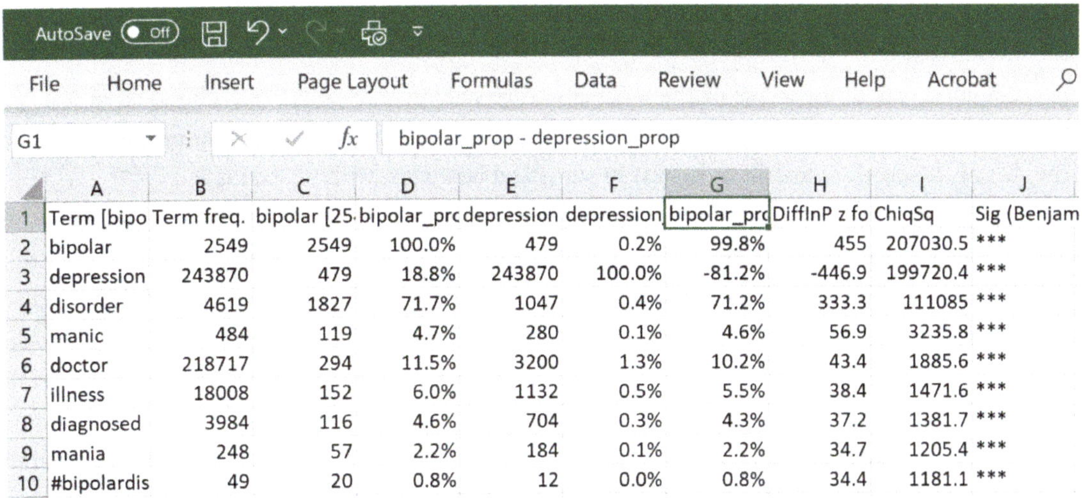

	A	B	C	D	E	F	G	H	I	J
1	Term [bipo	Term freq.	bipolar [25	bipolar_prc	depression	depression	bipolar_prc	DiffInP z fo	ChiqSq	Sig (Benjam
2	bipolar	2549	2549	100.0%	479	0.2%	99.8%	455	207030.5	***
3	depression	243870	479	18.8%	243870	100.0%	-81.2%	-446.9	199720.4	***
4	disorder	4619	1827	71.7%	1047	0.4%	71.2%	333.3	111085	***
5	manic	484	119	4.7%	280	0.1%	4.6%	56.9	3235.8	***
6	doctor	218717	294	11.5%	3200	1.3%	10.2%	43.4	1885.6	***
7	illness	18008	152	6.0%	1132	0.5%	5.5%	38.4	1471.6	***
8	diagnosed	3984	116	4.6%	704	0.3%	4.3%	37.2	1381.7	***
9	mania	248	57	2.2%	184	0.1%	2.2%	34.7	1205.4	***
10	#bipolardis	49	20	0.8%	12	0.0%	0.8%	34.4	1181.1	***

Figure 3.7: The Mozdeh *Association mining comparisons* tab results for the queries bipolar and depression copied into Excel. Three proportions columns have been formatted as percentages in Excel. All the terms shown here are more likely to occur in one than the other of bipolar and depression tweets.

For a WAD test to compare filters (e.g., sentiment, retweet counts), follow the instructions in the "Association mining comparisons" tab about how to add these to the query. If the comparison is male against female, then enter the query (only one query, or none) and check the "Compare male vs female" option before clicking the "Compare words matching the above queries…" button.

3.3 STATISTICAL DETAILS

Some statistical tests are necessary to reduce the chance of drawing false conclusions from WAD results. These tests are conducted automatically by Mozdeh for each WAD and this section explains how the tests work and where to find the test output.

Statistical tests are needed because the term lists produced by WAD may include terms by accident that do not reflect underlying trends. For example, suppose that a set of bipolar tweets is compared to a set of depression tweets. If the word "house" is in 3.3% of bipolar tweets but 3.2% of depression tweets, then this 0.1% difference might have occurred by accident (e.g., because one person with depression happened to tweet about the house they were in) rather than reflecting a genuine topic difference between bipolar disorder and depression tweeting.

How big a percentage difference is necessary to be sure that a percentage difference is not a fluke? It depends on the number of texts. If there are millions, then even a 0.1% difference is unlikely to occur by chance, whereas if there are 5 then a 40% difference (2 tweets) can easily occur by accident. A statistical test can report the likelihood that a difference has occurred by chance, avoiding the need for guesswork. Mozdeh uses two tests for the difference between the two percentages.

The first, not discussed here, is a difference between proportions test. The second, described below, is a chi-squared test.

A chi-squared test is one of the most common statistical tests. A "2×2" chi-squared test can be used to check whether it is likely that one percentage is different from another purely by chance. The rest of this section describes the test in statistical language, with an example.

Suppose that a word association detection run in Mozdeh has a collection of 10,000 tweets about Covid-19, with 8,000 of them during the first UK lockdown and 2,000 tweets from after this lockdown was eased. Mozdeh is trying to find words that are more common in the after lockdown tweets than in the during lockdown tweets. To do this, it will check every word in the after lockdown tweets individually. For each word, it will calculate the number of before lockdown tweets containing the word and the number of after lockdown tweets containing the word (Table 3.6). Suppose that it gets to the word "hug", finding it in 80 tweets from during lockdown and 200 after lockdown tweets. Then,

- "hug" is in 80/8,000 × 100% = 1% of during lockdown tweets, and
- "hug" is in 200/2,000 × 100% = 10% of after lockdown tweets.

It is clear that "hug" was more likely to be in tweets after lockdown but is the difference between 1% and 10% unlikely to have happened by accident? For a chi-squared test, this translates into asking if Table 3.6 is more biased than could be explained by chance. Another way of looking at this is to consider that 2.8% of the complete set of tweets contain "hug." How likely is it that, purely by chance, the during lockdown percentage was 1% and the after-lockdown percentage was 10%, given this overall average?

Table 3.6: A cross-tabulation of tweets containing "hug" during and after lockdown, as used in a 2×2 chi-squared test

Tweets	Contain "hug"	Don't Contain "hug"	Total
During lockdown	80 (1%)	7,920	8,000
After lockdown	200 (10%)	1,800	2,000
Total	**280 (2.8%)**	**9,720**	**10,000**

The chi-squared test calculates the probability that the table could have appeared by chance if there was no difference in the likelihood of people using the word "hug" in their tweet during or after lockdown. The result is in the form of a "p-value". This reports that the likelihood of the table occurring if there is no difference is probability p or less. How low do we want p to be to be safe to use the results? The agreement in statistics is that $p = 0.05$ is the maximum, and we should ignore the result if p is bigger than this. In fact, there are three levels of increasing security in the result, as follows.

- **$p \le 0.05$:** standard significance level, sometimes interpreted as "some evidence" of a difference—less than a 1 in 20 chance of incorrectly deducing that there is an underlying difference, when there isn't. This can be marked with a single star, "*".

- **$p \le 0.01$:** careful significance level, sometimes interpreted as "strong evidence" of a difference—less than a 1 in 100 chance of incorrectly deducing that there is an underlying difference, when there isn't. This can be marked with two stars, "**".

- **$p \le 0.001$:** very careful significance level, sometimes interpreted as "very strong evidence" of a difference—less than a 1 in 1000 chance of incorrectly deducing that there is an underlying difference, when there isn't. This can be marked with three stars, "***".

Using the above star notation, if the Mozdeh output for a WAD produced the following list, then there is very strong evidence that people were more likely to tweet about hugs after lockdown and some evidence that they were more likely to tweet about kisses after lockdown, but there is insufficient evidence to claim that tongues were more likely to be tweeted about after lockdown (no stars).

- Hug*** (10% after lockdown, 1% during lockdown)
- Kiss* (4% after lockdown, 2% during lockdown)
- Tongues (2% after lockdown, 1% during lockdown)

3.3.1 THEORETICAL ASSUMPTIONS

The statistical tests described above are based on two theoretical assumptions. The tests use inferential statistics designed for small samples taken from much larger populations. These tests typically infer unknown properties of the entire population from the properties of a small random sample. For example, to test if retired UK citizens are more concerned about Covid-19 than working UK citizens, a researcher might ask a random sample of 400, finding that 40% of the retired are worried and 30% of the working citizens. From this, the exact percentages of the whole of the UK are known but could be estimated at 40% and 30% from this sample. A statistical test would then reveal how likely it is that the whole population percentages really are different based on the two sample percentages.

In contrast to the above case, social web data sets are often almost complete so there is no random sample to draw inferences about. For example, a dataset might be essentially all UK tweets about Covid-19 during a specified month. For the purposes of the statistical test, the assumption must be made that these tweets are a sample from the assumed theoretical population of all tweets that could be made under similar circumstances. If a WAD found a statistically significant gender difference for a word and nothing changed, then a similar result would be extremely likely the next month even though all the texts would be different. This is related to a Heraclitus saying, "You could not step twice into the same river; for other waters are ever flowing on to you." The new tweets each day are different but statistically significant patterns should keep occurring unless something that influences them changes.

The second theoretical assumption is that the words in each text are independent of the words in the others. In particular, if users copy texts from other users or if there are multiple texts from the same user that has a consistent writing style or set of interests, then this independence assumption is violated. In practice, it is impossible to be sure that this is true, but the chances of copying can be reduced by allowing a maximum of one text per user removing identical tweets/retweets (these are options in Mozdeh).

The independence assumption is also violated by common phrases because the use of one word in such a phrase makes the use of another word from the phrase more likely. To give an extreme example, the use of the words "hoist" and "petard" are not independent because a tweet containing one is likely to contain the other due to the Shakespearean phrase "hoist with his own petard" combining both of these otherwise rare terms. There is no solution to this problem because language meaning relies on patterns of word use. Also because of this, the number of words matching a theme (as found by the thematic analysis part of WATA) is not a robust indicator of the importance of the theme.

3.3.2 EFFECT SIZES

WAD identifies words that occur more in one subset than another but does not tell you how important this difference is. For example, if *cosplay* occurs in 0.1% of UK tweets but 0.2% of U.S. tweets then this 0.1% difference might seem too small to be important. In statistics, it is often important to consider the "effect size" of a difference and ignore differences that are too small to be of practical significance. In a focused collection of texts, it might be possible to ignore words when the percentage differences are too small to be important, and the researcher can decide on a suitable threshold.

For broad collections of texts, specifying a minimum difference may be unhelpful. In the above case, even though the UK-U.S. difference is only 0.1%, *cosplay* is twice as prevalent for the U.S. than the UK. Since the text collection is broad, the vast majority of texts are probably unrelated to the issues prompting mentions of *cosplay*. To illustrate this, suppose that *cosplay* is only mentioned in discussions of hobbies and hobbies make up 10% of the broad collection. In a sub-collection of the 10% purely hobby-related texts, *cosplay* would make up 2% of UK tweets and 2% of U.S. tweets, so the difference would be ten times bigger than before: 1%. This shows that the size of a difference in a broad collection of tweets is arbitrary and cannot be used for a simple threshold.

3.4 PROTECTION AGAINST ACCIDENTALLY FINDING IRRELEVANT WORDS

The statistical procedure above is effective at checking the evidence that differences in the use of words between two sets is unlikely to have occurred by chance, except for the non-independence issue mentioned above. Unfortunately, there is a second statistical problem. Statistical tests are designed to be carried out one at a time but Mozdeh tests each word, so may conduct millions of simultaneous tests. Even if there is only a 1 in a 1000 chance of making an error with each test, if Mozdeh makes 100,000 tests, then it could make 100 errors simply because of the high volume of tests. Fortunately, this issue can be resolved by considering the number of simultaneous tests and adjusting the chi-squared p-value calculation for this. There are many ways of making adjustments, but Mozdeh uses the Benjamini-Hochberg (1995) method and reports one two or three stars for each word that passes the statistical test. Thus, *words in lists produced by Mozdeh can be ignored when they do not have at least one star.*

The Benjamini–Hochberg method is a "familywise" error protection method. It ensures that the collective chance of incorrectly identifying a percentage difference as not being caused by chance is not greater than the p-value used. Thus, if there are 100 words that get one star after a Benjamini-Hochberg correction, then there is at most a 1 in 20 chance of making any mistakes: 19 times out of 20 *none* of the word associations will be due to chance.

3.5 SAMPLE SIZE REQUIREMENTS

The power of word association detection depends on the sample size: the number of texts. Depending on the nature of the texts, a few hundred is necessary to have any chance of identifying meaningful words, but at least a 100,000 may be needed to find any non-obvious word associations. It is therefore a big data technique. This has two side-effects.

First, the results of small-scale pilot tests are likely to be disappointing, returning no significant terms. Pilot testing is essential for practice and to understand the type of content of the texts to be analyzed but will not give insights into the likely results of a full-scale investigation.

Second, it is important at the research design stage to plan enough time for extensive data collection to get many texts, ideally at least 100,000, as mentioned above. This 100,000 texts recommendation is based on tweeting about a general topic: 10,000 texts may be enough if the topic is focused so that irrelevant or low-quality texts are rare.

3.6 LIMITATIONS

An important WAD limitation is that the texts analyzed should be almost exclusively in a single language. If there is a substantial language mix, then WAD can identify word differences that are due to language community differences rather than topic differences. Another important limitation is that the results can be influenced by language choices that obstruct the relationship between words and meaning. To illustrate this, if half of the texts in a sample discuss mothers but the authors use different terminology (e.g., mom, mum, mother, mummy, ma) then WAD tests would give separate results for each word, reducing the percentages and statistical significance of each. Similarly, the method works at the level of individual words and is less effective at detecting language differences in the use of phrases. While it may detect differences for the individual words within phrases, this is influenced by the extent to which the words in a phrase are also used in other contexts. For example, if the words *bank* and *England* were used within many contexts in a set of texts then it would be less likely that a WAD would identify differences in the prevalence of *bank* and *England* between two subsets, even if the phrase "Bank of England" occurred at a greater rate in one subset than the other.

As mentioned in the Introduction, while Mozdeh works in most international languages, it cannot cope with Chinese and other languages that do not have spaces between words. This is because WAD works by comparing word frequencies and if Mozdeh cannot split a text into its component words then it cannot function. This problem can be resolved if other software is used to split the original text into words before importing it into Mozdeh. This is called "word segmentation" in the terminology of computational linguistics and there is free software for this in some languages. Mozdeh can only help with this process for Japanese. For example, after this process, Mozdeh's WAD words for a Japanese-language word association comparison of highly retweeted tweets against less retweeted tweets found the words 日本 (Japan), 人 (man), 発売 (release), and メリークリスマス (merry Christmas) to associate with high retweet counts.

The WAD approach is likely to be less effective for languages that have many forms of the same word or many words with similar meanings. Although this occurs to some extent for English, it is more common in some other languages. Examples include Russian with its highly inflectional morphology and Turkish, which is a highly agglutinative language. Such languages can express similar meanings with many different word forms, undermining the word frequency comparisons that are the basis for WAD. This issue could be addressed by pre-processing texts in these languages to split words (Turkish) and lemmatize words into common core forms (Russian), feeding the results into Mozdeh for the WAD calculations.

3.7 SUMMARY

This chapter describes a word association detection test to find words that occur in a higher percentage of texts in one subset than another. The two subsets might consist of one subset and the remainder of the texts or might consist of two non-overlapping subsets, ignoring the remainder. The statistical tests described above help to ensure that it is unlikely that any of the WAD words are due to chance rather than difference in the underlying likelihood of using the words. WAD produces a list of words and statistical significance information (none, one, two or three stars). Words without at least one star can be ignored for having a reasonable likelihood of being the result of random variations.

This stage produces no information about what caused the words to be in the list and no information about what the words typically mean, when used, and the context in which they were used. These important omissions are the subject of the next chapter.

CHAPTER 4

Word Association Contextualization: Term Meaning and Context

As described in the previous chapter, word association detection produces a list of words that are more prevalent within one set of documents, such as tweets or comments, than another (Figure 4.1, 4.2). The next stage, word association contextualization (WAC), is to interpret the meaning of the words in the context of this difference: producing semantic descriptions or codes. For example, WAD might report that "care" was used in 2% of UK tweets in the second half of the 2020 Covid-19 lockdown but only 0.5% of UK tweets in the first half of the 2020 Covid-19 lockdown. This fact alone does not reveal what the difference signifies because the tweets could be about care homes, home-based informal care, caring about political decisions, or something else: different contexts.

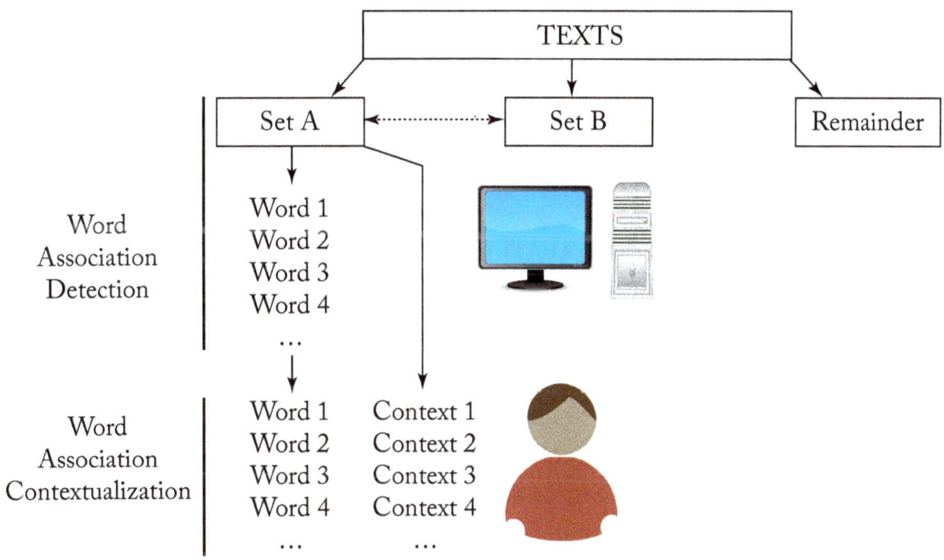

Figure 4.1: The WAD and WAC stages for comparing two subsets of a set of texts.

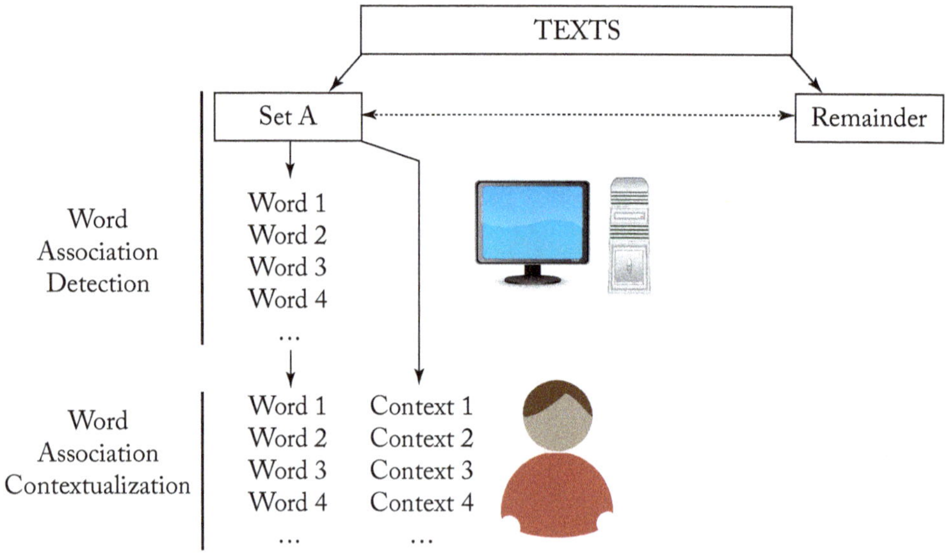

Figure 4.2: The WAD and WAC stages for comparing a subset of texts with the remaining texts.

For this chapter, a "word" is a continuous string of letters or characters, delimited by spaces or punctuation. Words include usernames, words in languages, such as Arabic, that do not use the Western alphabet, and made-up words, including typos. Within Mozdeh, words can include digits, hyphens, underscores and apostrophes but can't be just a number. For English, words are equated with their depluralized versions (removing any trailing "*s*").

The interpretation of individual WAD words might be relatively straightforward. If one of the words was "@GretaThunberg", then this implies that the Swedish environmental activist was referenced more in one set than the other, which is easy to interpret. In contrast, if one of the words was "Sarah" then it would be important to discover which Sarah(s) this referred to, otherwise the word on its own is close to meaningless. Similarly, suppose that one of the words was "Amritsar", a city in the Punjab, India. A tweet using this word might be a about a visit to the city, the importance of the Sikh Golden Temple of Amritsar, or the significance of the Amritsar massacre by the British Army of unarmed civilians in the city during the colonial era. Without knowing which Sarah or the context of the mentions of Amritsar, it would not be possible to draw general conclusions from the fact that these words are more common in one set of texts than another.

This chapter introduces methods to clarify the meaning and context of lists of WAD words. As the Sarah and Amritsar examples above illustrate, both meaning and context can be dependent on the texts analyzed. The methods introduced here don't work well with very general words like pronouns, conjunctions, and articles, which are discussed at the end of the next subsection.

4.1 WORD ASSOCIATION CONTEXTUALIZATION FROM A RANDOM SAMPLE OF RELEVANT TEXTS

The simplest WAC method to narrow down the meaning of a WAD word is to read a set of texts from the sample that contain it. This is a standard technique in linguistics, known as the key word in context (KWIC) method or concordance analysis (e.g., Bednarek, 2019). For example, if the word is "Sarah" and a sample of ten texts from the collection all mention Sarah Jessica Parker then the word "Sarah" can be interpreted as "Sarah Jessica Parker." Two levels of meaning may need to be detected: the meaning of the word and its typical context.

4.1.1 WORD ASSOCIATION CONTEXTUALIZATION OVERVIEW

This subsection gives an overview of the WAC process and the following subsections have additional details and definitions. WAC has three steps.

1. Create a random sample of texts containing the term within the specified subset in which is it most prevalent (e.g., female-authored or UK tweets). Instructions for this in Mozdeh are in the next subsection.

2. Read enough texts (see Table 4.1) to detect the word's typical meaning.

3. Read enough texts (see Table 4.1) to detect the word's typical context.

Table 4.1 gives guidelines about how many texts to read for this task. For example, if at least nine of the first ten texts suggest the same meaning and context, stop. Otherwise, if the first 20 texts give 80% the same meaning and context (i.e., 16–20) then stop. Otherwise, if the first 40 texts give 70% the same meaning and context (i.e., at least 28) then stop. Otherwise, try 80 and report the results, which might be that there are at least 2 different meanings and/or contexts. The guidelines can be violated for a pilot test (e.g., halve the number of texts) or made more stringent for important words or careful analyses (e.g., double the number of texts).

Table 4.1: The number of random texts to read to detect the meaning and context of a WAD word

Number of Texts	When to Choose
10	At least 90% of the texts give the same meaning and context.
20	At least 80% of the texts give the same meaning and context.
40	At least 70% of the texts give the same meaning and context.
80	Otherwise

Once meaning and context have been detected then the guidelines in Table 4.2 suggest how to report the results. These are not foolproof but provide a default range for reporting. Again, these can be relaxed for a pilot test or made more stringent by extra checks (word association subsections of this chapter) for more careful results.

Table 4.2: Guidelines about the meaning or context to report for a WAD word

Percentage of Texts	Meaning or Context to Report
66%+	The dominant meaning and context of the WAD word.
50%–66%	The dominant meaning and context unless there are two meaning and/or contexts in similar numbers of texts (one not more than double the number of texts than the other), in which case report both.
25%–49%	The dominant meaning and context unless there are other meanings and contexts in similar numbers of texts (all at least 25%), in which case report all these.
0%–24%	Report as "Multiple" or used advanced WAC methods.

The guidelines (Table 4.2) suggest reporting meanings and contexts that cover at least 25% of the texts analyzed. This can ignore a majority of the texts: 75% in the worst case. The rationale for this is as follows. If no common themes can be detected in the texts that are unaccounted for then it is likely that these texts are randomly distributed between the two subsets compared in the word association test. Thus, the word association found is likely to be due to the common theme rather than the remaining texts. This can be explicitly tested for in a follow-up word association test (see below).

4.1.2 CREATING THE WAC TEXT SAMPLE WITH MOZDEH

The sample of texts to be read can be created in two ways with Mozdeh: on screen and saved to file. To produce a randomly ordered list on screen for a WAD term with Mozdeh, enter the search term, select the filters used to generate the WAD list (e.g., gender), select the *Random sort order* in the *Sort by* drop-down box, and click Search. This displays a random list of about 40 matching texts underneath the buttons. More texts can be obtained by clicking the Next button afterward.

To illustrate the above process, suppose that a gender-based WAD had found *systemic* to be a female-associated text. A list of female-authored texts containing this word could be found by selecting the female filter, entering *systemic* as the query term, selecting *Random* in the *Sort By* box, and clicking *Search* (Figure 4.3). If a WAD involved keywords rather than filters, then the keyword should be added to the search text box, with the term AND. For example, if the term *systemic* had been found for a WAD based on the search term *racism* (i.e., the term *systemic* was more prevalent in racism tweets then the remainder), then the gender filter would not be needed but the search box should include *racism AND systemic* to ensure that matching texts would contain both terms.

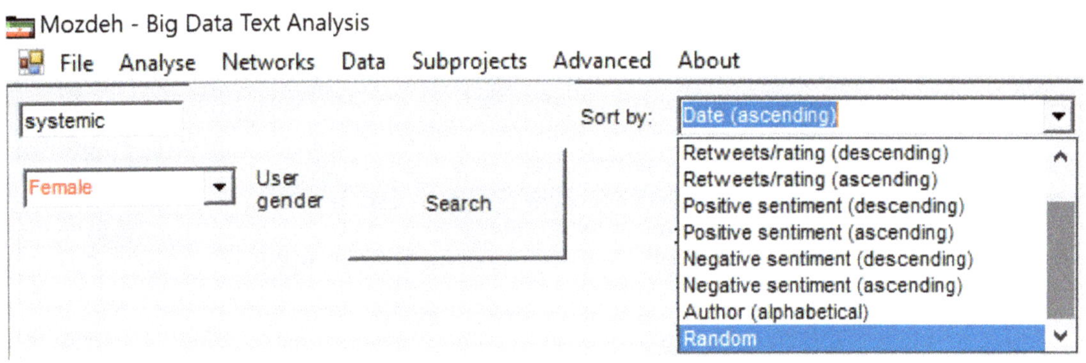

Figure 4.3: Mozdeh configured to display a random sample of female-authored texts containing the term systemic. The interface has been simplified to highlight relevant features. After clicking Search, random matching texts will be listed underneath.

A text file with random samples for all WAD words can be created in a single stage by Mozdeh instead of listed on screen. For this, select the appropriate filters (e.g., gender), and click the WATA button in the Save tab and select the WAD results file (Figure 4.4). This file can then be loaded into a spreadsheet to be read for the WAC interpretations (Figure 4.5).

If a single WAD file contains WAD terms from multiple filters (e.g., terms associated with males and females in the same file) then this process would need to be carried out twice, once for each filter. The WAC interpretations should use the relevant set. For example, if *systemic* was a female-associated word then the WAC file for the female filter should be used to contextualize this term, rather than the WAC file for the male filter.

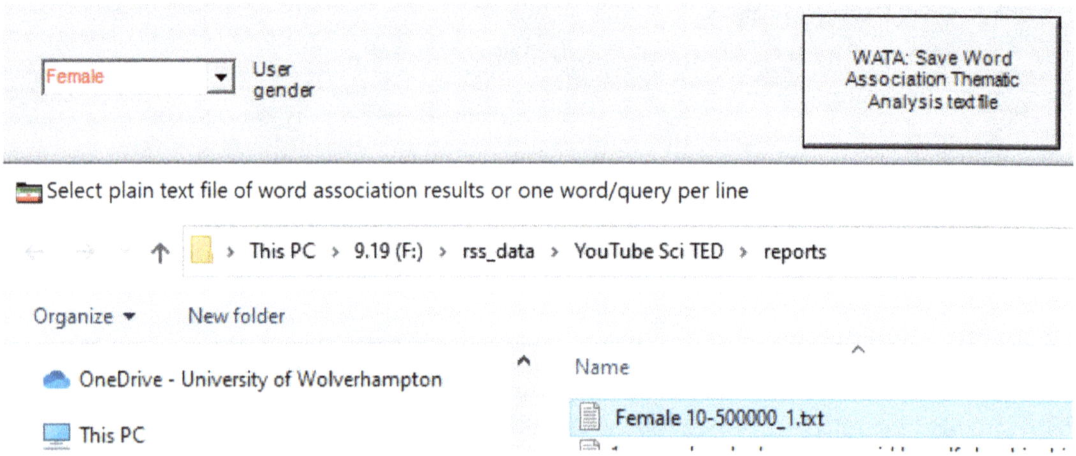

Figure 4.4: Mozdeh configured to save a file containing a random sample of female-authored texts containing all terms found by WAD. The interface has been simplified to highlight relevant features. After selecting the female filter (top left), clicking the WATA button (top right), and selecting the WAD file (Female 10-500000_1.txt), random matching texts will be saved to a new file.

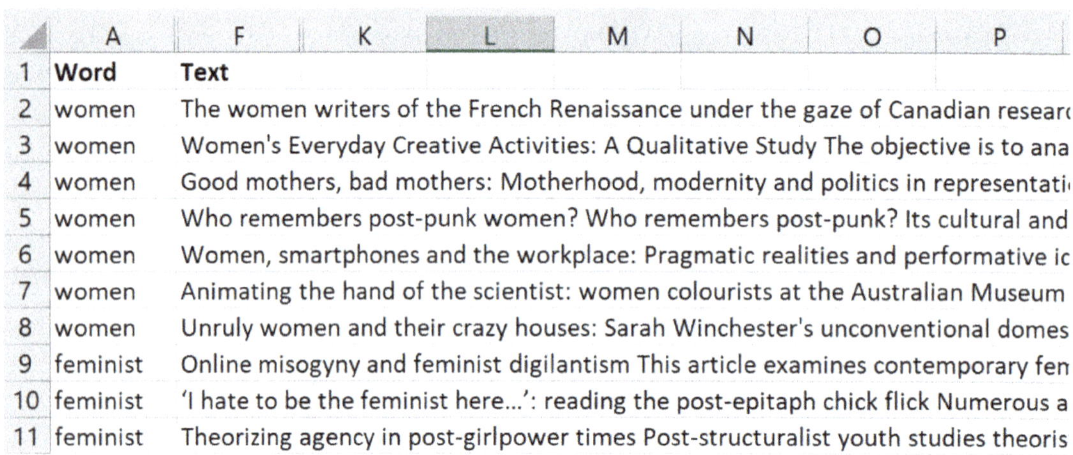

	A	F
1	**Word**	**Text**
2	women	The women writers of the French Renaissance under the gaze of Canadian researc
3	women	Women's Everyday Creative Activities: A Qualitative Study The objective is to ana
4	women	Good mothers, bad mothers: Motherhood, modernity and politics in representati
5	women	Who remembers post-punk women? Who remembers post-punk? Its cultural and
6	women	Women, smartphones and the workplace: Pragmatic realities and performative ic
7	women	Animating the hand of the scientist: women colourists at the Australian Museum
8	women	Unruly women and their crazy houses: Sarah Winchester's unconventional domes
9	feminist	Online misogyny and feminist digilantism This article examines contemporary fen
10	feminist	'I hate to be the feminist here...': reading the post-epitaph chick flick Numerous a
11	feminist	Theorizing agency in post-girlpower times Post-structuralist youth studies theoris

Figure 4.5: The file created by the WATA button in Mozdeh copied to a spreadsheet and tidied. This is for a list of female-associated terms within a set of visual arts texts. The WAD words are in the Word column and the random texts matching a female filter are in the Text column.

4.1.3 DETECTING TYPICAL MEANINGS FOR POLYSEMOUS WORDS AND WORDS IN EXPRESSIONS

The meaning of many words depends on how they are used, especially if the same word can mean multiple things or if it is used in a multi-word expression or name. It is helpful to define this term precisely in the context of the method, since it is nonstandard terminology.

Definition: The ***meaning*** of a WAD word is its dictionary definition meaning. For a word with multiple dictionary definition meanings, its meaning is the definition that most closely matches the way it is used in the texts. If the word is almost always used in the context of a given phrase, then its meaning is instead that of the phrase containing it. Here, dictionary definition should be interpreted loosely rather than tied to a given dictionary.

The typical meaning of each WAD word should be detected by reading a random sample of texts containing it (e.g., Figure 4.3), obtained as described above. For many words, the meaning will be obvious. For example, the word *skirl* is only ever used to describe the sound of a bagpipe so its meaning is always the same. In contrast, words that have multiple potential meanings or occur mainly in phrases need to be investigated to identify the meaning that typically applies in the samples. For example, a word like *love* can mean romantic love ("Do you love me?"), liking ("I love the red shoes!"), or no score in tennis ("she led thirty love"). Similarly, the word nurse could mean the job, feeding a baby, or looking after someone.

A word might also occur in WAD results because it is within a fixed expression, such as a proper noun or saying. For instance, the term *breaking* might occur because it is commonly used to discuss the TV series Breaking Bad, so in this case the meaning of the term *breaking* would be the Breaking Bad TV series. While technically the meaning of the term *breaking* here is "learning how to be (bad)", if it is almost exclusively used to refer to the TV series, then its underlying meaning is the TV series as part of its name.

The above can be illustrated with the example of *Sarah*. Suppose that a word association test had found the word *Sarah* to have been used more by females than males in a collection of tweets about news. Mozdeh could be used, as above, to produce a randomly sorted set of female-authored texts containing the term *Sarah*, as in the made-up tweets below.

__Sarah__ Jessica Parker is on Late Night Live tonight!!!
Can't believe __Sarah__ Jessica Parker finally agreed to Sex in the City 3.
My mum loves __Sarah__ Jessica Parker and is dragging me to her new film.
Would love to see that __Sarah__ whatshername off of Sex in the City at the premiere!

If the *Sarah* referenced in the first 10 is Sarah Jessica Parker then she could be taken as the meaning of *Sarah* in this context: females mention Sarah Jessica Parker more than do males (assuming that males don't call her something else, such as Parker or SJP).

In the above example, if some tweets mentioned Sarah Jessica Parker and some mentioned UK comedian Sarah Millican then more tweets would need to be checked to find which is more common in the complete set. If they are both common, then the word would have to be assigned a double meaning: Sarah Jessica Parker and Sarah Millican.

Sarah Millican: My New Year's resolution is to get in shape… I choose round.
When it comes to life and love, why do we believe our worst reviews? ***Sarah*** Jessica Parker
Sarah Jessica Parker never dreamt of a wedding day and the birth of a first child
Spend the evening home alone to guarantee yourself sex says ***Sarah*** Millican

Words that are not proper nouns can also have multiple meanings (polysemy) so their main meaning still needs to be detected. For example, in the list below, the term has two meanings, "dating" and "understanding" so if it is in a list of word association terms then the most common meaning needs to be detected because it would make a substantial difference to any conclusions drawn (e.g., females discussed romance more than males; or females were more analytical than males).

You ***seeing*** *him yet? Go girl.*

I'm not ***seeing*** *why anyone would think COVID-19 B.1.1.7, 20I/501Y.V1 should resist current vaccines, based on the location of the mutations.*

4.1.4 IDENTIFYING WORD CONTEXTS

The typical context for a word might be narrower than its meaning. For example, when discovering that the *Sarah* term is Sarah Jessica Parker, it might be clear that she is almost always discussed in the context of one event, such as a film opening or fashion launch. In this case the Sarah Jessica Parker meaning of *Sarah* might be narrowed down further to the context of *Sarah* being, "Sarah Jessica Parker at the opening night of the film Sex in the City 3". This should be helpful when trying to draw conclusions from the term.

Definition: The **context** of a WAD word refers to the setting, if any, in which it is typically used in the texts analyzed. The context of a WAD word can only be deduced from reading the surrounding text to check its purpose and role. It is either the same as its meaning (as defined above) or is narrower if this meaning is employed in one or a few related settings.

The value of context information is illustrated by the following series of increasingly precise conclusions that might be drawn from *Sarah* being mentioned more by females than by males.

- Females tweeted the word Sarah more than did males.
- Females tweeted about actress Sarah Jessica Parker more than did males.
- Females mentioned Sarah Jessica Parker at the opening night of the film Sex in the City 3 more than did males.

Context can be identified from the random sample in a similar way as detecting meaning, and at the same time. Detecting context involves answering the question, "What is the common setting for most uses of this term?" The answer should be as specific as consistent with the data, but no more. In some cases, a context may be so general that it coincides with the meaning. For example, if tweets about Benedict Cumberbatch commented on a wide range of aspects of his life then it would not be possible to obtain a narrower context from these mentions of his name. In contrast, the following tweets have a common context for the term "hot".

*It was hot hot **hot** today so I chilled at the beach.*
*Tooooo **hot** to work so read a book in the garden.*
*This **hot** weather is great for the roses.*

The common context for these tweets is hot weather, in contrast to the tweets below, where the term has the same meaning (high temperature) but a different context.

*The samosas were even tastier when they were **hot**!*
*Fresh rolls, **hot** out the oven. Yummity yum yum.*
***Hot** apple pie for real!?!—I'll be is your slave forever.*

The context of a word can be much more specific than could be guessed without reading a random sample of texts, so this step should not be omitted or rushed. For example, a study of gender differences in commenting on museum videos found the term pee to be female-associated (Thelwall, 2018c). The WAC for this word found that its context was the difficulty in peeing for rich women in 18th century Britain wearing multiple layers of fashionable clothes. This could not be guessed without reading the comments.

4.1.5 DIFFICULT CASES: PRONOUNS AND STYLISTIC WORDS

The random sample method works best when there is an easily identifiable common context in a word's random sample. This may be difficult for pronouns: if females are found to use the term "she" more often, then reading random samples may reveal many different settings. These may be associated with a style of writing or broad focus (e.g., a greater interest in women) rather than a narrow context. Here are some suggestions for the types of context that pronouns may represent.

- **I, me, my, myself, mine:** discussing personal issues, actions, or opinions.
- **You, you're, your, yourself:** participating in a dialog or argument with a person or group.
- **She, her, herself:** a focus on women, girls, or females in general (unless used for pets, ships, or objects).
- **He, him, his:** a focus on men, boys, or males in general (unless used for pets).

- **It, itself (also: the):** a focus on information (and away from people).
- **We, our, ourselves, us:** discussing group issues, actions, or opinions.
- **They, them, their, themselves (also: people):** discussing or generalizing about others (e.g., "people don't trust politicians")

To illustrate how the above list could be used to draw conclusions, suppose that a word association list for a set of tweets about Covid-19 had included the terms "she," "her," "him" for females and "people," "it" for males. Then it could be concluded that female-authored tweets were more likely to focus on individual males and females (perhaps generalizing this to a focus on individual people in a follow-up thematic analysis) whereas male-authored tweets were more likely to be informational or make generalizations about populations (e.g., "people need to stop going to beaches on sunny days during lockdown").

Words can sometimes also perform a stylistic function that may not be obvious from reading a random sample of texts. Here are some examples from previous studies where the cause of the difference in use of the terms seems to be stylistic.

- **Omg:** a stylistically female word expressing surprise (either females express surprise more in text, use this word more than males, or both, I am not sure).
- **Swear words:** a stylistically male word choice usually expressing negative sentiment (either males express negativity more or use swear words to express it more: I don't know why males seem more willing to use certain swear words on Twitter.
- **And, but, because:** complex sentence constructions, or longer texts.

Caution should be used when drawing conclusions from words that are strong stylistically gendered because any gender differences found in them may be stylistic rather than based on their content. For example, if *omg* was found to be a female-associated word in a WAD then it would not be reasonable to conclude that females expressed surprise more because males may have used alternative terminology.

4.1.6 RANDOM SAMPLE SUMMARY

As discussed in this subsection, the purpose of reading a random sample of texts is to detect first the meaning and second the context of each term in a word association list from the WAD stage. Recall that the meaning of a WAD word may be either a dictionary definition meaning of the word or may be the phrase containing the word, if it is usually within a fixed phrase. In contrast, the context of a WAD word is the setting in which the word is usually employed within the random texts.

The tasks of identifying the meaning and context of a word may be straightforward or difficult, depending on the word or the random set of texts. Some examples are given in Table 4.3 to illustrate the range of difficulty levels that may be faced. The contexts of the more difficult words needs to be interpreted carefully.

Table 4.3: Examples of problems of interpretation for words found by word association analyses. Terms higher in the table are likely to be easier to interpret

Word	Possible Meanings	Possible Narrower Contexts for the First Meaning
Skirl	The sound of bagpipes	A specific musical event; a specific song
@GretaThunberg	The environmental leader Greta Thunberg	Environmental issues; press attacks on Greta Thunberg; a comment by Greta Thunberg
Stormzy	The British rapper Stormzy	A Stormzy song release; an initiative from Stormzy
Environment	Environmental issues; surroundings of something	Global warming; sea level rises; a weather event; an environmental campaign
Amritsar	The city of Amritsar; the Amritsar massacre; the Golden Temple of Amritsar	The city itself; tourism in Amritsar; an election in Amritsar; Operation Blue Star; Amritsar textiles
Sarah	Sarah Jessica Parker; Sarah Millican; the baby name Sarah	Sarah Jessica Parker's career; a particular Sarah Jessica Parker film
Wonderful	Very good; The film, "It's a Wonderful Life"	A wonderful concert; a wonderful museum; appreciation for the videos discussed
She	The personal pronoun she	A focus on women; a focus on females; a focus on boats
We	The personal pronoun we	A tendency to focus on the actions or opinions of a group; a personal focus
The	Indefinite article	A tendency to focus on information or things
And	Conjunction	Complex sentence construction; longer texts

4.2 ADVANCED WORD ASSOCIATION CONTEXTUALIZATION

The results from reading a random sample of texts for WAC, as above, may be ambiguous when no single context for a word dominates the results. This section introduces some advanced methods to deal with this problem. These advanced methods are time consuming and so should be used when WAD finds few words, so each one is important, or when there is another reason to take extra care with each term's WAC. If there are plenty of terms from WAD and there is no special reason to ensure that each one is fully analyzed, then the ambiguous terms can be classified as "Multiple" and effectively ignored. In such cases, the methods in this section are not needed.

4.2.1 FOLLOW-UP WORD ASSOCIATION DETECTION FOR THE TERM

The random sample method may not give clear results when a word is used in many different contexts, with perhaps some of the contexts being similar. In this case, a follow-up word association detection for the selected term can suggest its most common contexts. For example, suppose that the term 5G (a cellular network communication technology) was identified by a date-based WAD applied to Covid-19 tweets as being more prevalent in March–April 2020 than later. Consider the three (two false) texts below about 5G from this set of Covid-19 tweets.

__5G__ disrupts oxygenation of hemoglobin in the blood.
__5G__ to revolutionize the global mobile services industry
Covid-19 caused by __5G__—it's a mobile phone company conspiracy

A common context is not clear from these tweets, so it may help to identify words that are more prevalent in 5G tweets than in the remaining tweets. If a list of words that are more prevalent in 5G tweets than in other tweets includes some that suggest common themes, then this information could be used to deduce a common context. This list can be produced by a follow-up WAD of the term 5G from the original date-based WAD (i.e., a topic WAD based on the keyword 5G, using the terminology of the WAD chapter).

To illustrate the value of this method, a follow-up WAD for the term 5G in a set of Covid-19 tweets gives the results in Table 4.4. The most common term (highest match percentage) here is *cause*, with a score of 29.1% (compared to 0.6% for tweets not containing cause). Thus, 29.1% of tweets containing 5G also contain *cause*, so probably about 29% of tweets talk about 5G causing something. Reading a random sample of tweets containing both 5G and *cause* would find that these tweets often mentioned 5G being (incorrectly) hypothesized to cause Covid-19 by supposedly disrupting the human oxygen intake mechanism. Other tweets mention 5G towers being attacked, protected, or vandalized. The context common to both is the false hypothesis that 5G causes Covid-19. Two of the terms (*4G* and fifth-generation) have very strong associations with 5G but are rare enough to ignore (occurring in under 1% of 5G tweets, according to the table). Thus, Table 4.4

suggests that claims about 5G causing Covid-19 is the appropriate WAD context for the term 5G in the Covid-19 tweets.

Table 4.4: A follow-up WAD showing words associating with "5G" in a collection of Covid-19 tweets

Word	In 5G Tweets %	In Other Tweets %	In 5G Tweets	In All Tweets	Chisq	Sig
5G	100.0%	0.0%	573	573	17704626	***
4G	0.9%	0.0%	5	35	17899	***
absorbing	2.3%	0.0%	13	291	16595	***
tower	9.2%	0.0%	53	7475	11313	***
radiation	6.6%	0.0%	38	4133	10459	***
cause	29.1%	0.6%	167	112843	7321	***
vandalize	0.5%	0.0%	3	36	5369	***
fifth-generation	0.3%	0.0%	2	13	5354	***
conspiracy	13.8%	0.2%	79	34746	5344	***

The 25% guideline is recommended again here: if a meaning/concept covers at least 25% of the texts and the remainder do not seem to follow a theme, then the main meaning/concept can be reported, with the assumption that the texts not following a pattern are likely to be randomly distributed between the two sets used for the original word association test. The 25% can be checked against the original random sample and can include all synonyms and phrases with the same meaning/context for this check.

If the follow-up WAD does not produce any terms with a matching percentage above 25% then it might be possible to find a set of related terms (e.g., synonyms) that collectively add up to above 25% and use the concept behind them. For example, combining "COVID-19" and "coronavirus" from Table 4.5 contains an estimated 26.3% + 28.7% = 55% (ignoring overlaps) of tweets mentioning the disease. Thus, and noting the personal pronouns in the table, the term "scared" is likely to be typically used in the context of admitting fear about Covid-19, although this should be checked against the random sample.

Table 4.5: A follow-up WAD showing words associating with "scared" in a collection of Covid-19 tweets

Word	In scared tweets %	Not in scared tweets %	In scared tweets	In all tweets	Chisq	Sig
scared	100.0%	0.0%	16808	16808	7446333	***
shitless	0.8%	0.0%	129	145	50308	***
I'm	9.8%	1.2%	1639	92167	9988	***
im	4.0%	0.2%	672	18811	9379	***
I	35.6%	12.5%	5981	932345	8181	***
luscious	0.1%	0.0%	25	44	6008	***
coronavirus	26.3%	9.1%	4419	680613	5967	***
am	8.3%	1.4%	1403	103442	5954	***
my	22.4%	7.1%	3763	529585	5951	***
COVID-19	28.7%	10.8%	4823	806162	5571	***
but	19.6%	6.4%	3291	480575	4808	***

In Mozdeh, the follow-up WAD above can be run by clearing all filters, entering the term in the main search box and clicking the *Mine associations for search and filters* button.

4.2.2 FOLLOW-UP WORD ASSOCIATION DETECTION WITHIN TEXTS CONTAINING THE TERM

If the random sample and follow-up WAD methods do not give positive results, then a third method can be tried. This is to detect words associating with the chosen term in its set compared to the other set. For example, if the term *ppl* (people) is in a WAD list of words more used by males than by females, what is the context for this difference? If both males and females use the term a lot, then the context that is more prevalent for males can be detected by examining the words that occur more in male-authored tweets containing *ppl* than in female-authored tweets containing *ppl*. *This method detects when a term is used in many contexts, but the word association results are due to one of these contexts being relatively more common for one of the two sets compared (e.g., females) compared to the other (e.g., males).*

From Table 4.6, when males tweet about Covid-19 with the term *ppl* there are nine terms that they more likely to use terms than females, with two terms in the opposite direction. These terms partly group into a financial set (bitcoin, bank, trade) but the rest do not clearly group together. To investigate whether they fit together, male-authored tweets containing them together with the term *ppl* should be examined. For example, tweets containing *sir* and *ppl* are often tweets to the Prime Minister of India, Narendra Damodardas Modi. This is also true for *govt* and *@pmoindia*, giving an Indian politics context for males using *ppl*. The same strategy reveals that the terms *Iran* and *avoid* are also used by males in the context of discussing international trade deals. Thus, the male association with the term *ppl* has two contexts: males being more likely to tweet to Indian politicians, and males being more likely to tweet about the finance of international trade (or one aspect of it, at least).

Table 4.6: A follow-up WAD showing words associating with males for the term "*ppl*" in a collection of Covid-19 tweets

Term	Frequency	ppl<M>	ppl<M> %	ppl<F>	ppl<F> %	ppl<M>% - ppl<F>%	ChiqSq	Sig
my	529585	267	6.9%	407	11.6%	-4.7%	48.7	***
sir	44003	83	2.1%	13	0.4%	1.8%	45.2	***
govt	45885	160	4.1%	55	1.6%	2.6%	43	***
bc	21962	69	1.8%	153	4.4%	-2.6%	41.7	***
India	72744	88	2.3%	19	0.5%	1.7%	38.7	***
trade	9764	46	1.2%	3	0.1%	1.1%	34	**
I	932345	776	20.1%	902	25.7%	-5.6%	33.1	**
bitcoin	1605	44	1.1%	3	0.1%	1.1%	32.2	**
bank	28116	69	1.8%	14	0.4%	1.4%	31.8	**
@pmoindia	27463	61	1.6%	11	0.3%	1.3%	30.4	*
Iran	12022	48	1.2%	6	0.2%	1.1%	29	*
avoid	30075	74	1.9%	19	0.5%	1.4%	27.9	*

In the above example, all the terms have low percentages. The highest term for males, *govt*, occurred in 4.1% of male-authored tweets containing *ppl*. This is much lower than the 25% minimum that previous methods have used. This is acceptable here because the test is a direct test of difference between males and females. The assumption here, supported by the table, is that other terms are used to a similar degree by males and females and so are not the cause of the gender difference found for *ppl*: it is only due to males being more likely to tweet about financial trade and to Indian politicians.

In Mozdeh, a word association analysis can be run by clearing all filters and search terms, selecting the Association mining comparisons tab, and entering the two queries to compare in the association mining comparisons text box, separated by a comma. In the above case, there is a special checkbox for comparisons, so only the single word needs to be entered, as follows:

ppl

The "Compare male vs. female for each query" option should also be checked. After this, click the *Compare words matching the above queries…* button. The results (words that are disproportionately often used by males or females in tweets containing *ppl*) will be saved in a plain text file (ending in "_diffp") that can be loaded into Excel to read.

4.3 WORD ASSOCIATION CONTEXTUALIZATION TEST ASSUMPTIONS

There are two types of assumption underlying the above three tests. The first two tests (random sample reading, and advanced follow-up [standard] word association detection) attempt to detect the main meaning and context of a term within *all* texts mentioning the term. The assumption behind these tests is that the difference between sets is due to the main meaning or context found rather than the other contexts (Figure 4.6, top).

In contrast, the follow-up word association analysis within texts containing the term avoids this assumption by directly checking for terms that are more common in one set than another (Figure 4.6, bottom). The assumption here is that the difference is due to one or a small number of meanings and contexts and that the remaining meanings/contexts are evenly distributed between the two sets.

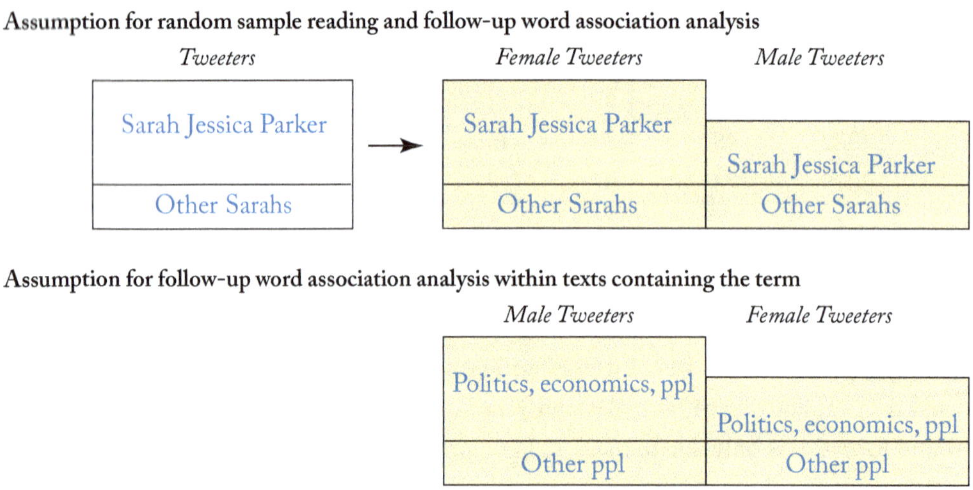

Figure 4.6: Assumptions underlying three of the tests used to detect meaning and context of individual terms. In the top case, the top left set (all tweeters) is examined and the assumption is that the dominant topic within the set of tweets containing the term (e.g., *Sarah*) is the cause of the term (i.e., *Sarah*) occurring more in one subset (e.g., female-authored tweets) than the other. In the bottom case, the test directly checks for meanings/contexts for which the term (e.g., *ppl*) is more common in one set (e.g., male-authored tweets) than the other, and the assumption is that the remaining contexts of the term (*ppl*) are evenly distributed between the two sets.

In terms of the Figure 4.4 example, the assumption illustrated at the top of the figure is that finding the dominant meaning/context of the term *Sarah* will reveal the cause of the gender difference in its use. So, if *Sarah* usually refers to Sarah Jessica Parker, then the reason why females tweet *Sarah* more than males tweet *Sarah* is that females are more likely to tweet about Sarah Jessica Parker. This assumption is not needed for the bottom of Figure 4.1, because the test directly finds that the term *ppl* is used more by males than by females in the context of *politics* and *economics*. The only assumption here is that these two contexts (politics and economics) are the cause of the statistically significant gender difference in the use of the term *ppl*, because other contexts for *ppl* are approximately evenly distributed between males and females.

4.4 CAUSES OF WORD ASSOCIATIONS: NEWS, VIRAL SHARING, OR SOCIETAL DIFFERENCES?

The statistical tests used for WAD, as described above, are designed to minimize the possibility of incorrectly claiming that a term has an association when it doesn't. The WAC stage then identifies the meaning and context of the difference. Nevertheless, the results do not give any information about the *underlying cause* of the results, and there are at least five types: spam/bots, date, news, viral sharing, and societal differences. These are illustrated here, with examples.

Suppose that a WAD of Covid-19 tweets compared subset A, tweets in May, with subset B, tweets in March, to find terms that were more prevalent in March tweets than May tweets. Suppose that the results included five statistically significant terms: *prize*, *March*, *Italy*, *dogs*, and *frightened*. These illustrate the five different types of cause.

- **Spam and bots**: Widespread online marketing campaigns or bot tweets might result in terms in the WAD lists, when not detected and blocked by Twitter. Mozdeh attempts to reduce the likelihood of this occurring by removing similar tweets (e.g., the same text but different hashtags). Any spam or bot-related terms should be ignored. In the above example, the word association for *prize* was due to a smartphone app running a Twitter competition for users to tweet a screenshot of a picture taken with the app.

- **Date-related terms:** A WAD for subsets of texts from two different periods might include date-related terms, such as weekdays, years, or month names. These are not informative and can be ignored. In the above example, *March* is an irrelevant date term.

- **News events:** There is a substantial amount of news-related tweeting and so words in news stories are likely to be prominent in date-based WAD results. Italy was the first European country to have a major Covid-19 outbreak and was extensively discussed in the Western press in March, causing *Italy* to be a significant term in the March vs. May Covid-19 WAD. This directly reflects press coverage and indirectly reflects the events discussed. More specifically, it reflects world or local events through the (distorting) selection and reporting lens of the media.

- **Viral spreading:** Some non-news topics, such as memes and jokes, are extensively discussed in short bursts. Words associated with these jokes or memes are likely to be prominent in date-based WAD results. In March, jokes were shared about the World Health Organization (WHO) announcing that pets did not need to be kept inside because they were unlikely to spread Covid-19. This resulted in the viral spreading of jokes with the punchline "WHO let the dogs out." Thus, the prevalence of *dogs* reflects an arguably minor world event but is primarily due to someone realizing the coincidence of the event with a popular song.

- **Societal differences:** Some words may reflect differences in opinions or topics between the two sets. The greater use of the term *frightened* in March compared to May probably reflects greater fear at the start of the pandemic than later, when many people had lived through several months of it and had not felt an immediate daily threat.

Because of the multiple possible causes of positive WAD results, it is important to check for likely causes when making inferences from them. To illustrate this, it would be misleading to claim that the population became less interested in dogs because of Covid-19 based on the term *dog* being rarer in May tweets than March tweets because the change had a viral rather than societal cause. Claims about societal differences should not be made if the WAC stage reveals another explanation. The motivating research questions should also be considered at this stage because they may influence the types of cause that may be relevant.

4.5 USING MULTIPLE CODERS

Word association contextualization is subjective and partly dependant on the general knowledge of the coder. The validity of the results can therefore be improved by using more than one coder, comparing the results between coders and producing an agreed meaning and context for each term. This is important if some of the terms are difficult to find contexts for and there are not many terms. It can be achieved in two ways.

The first coder could conduct the procedures above, passing the results and texts (the random sample for each term created with Mozdeh's WATA button in the Save tab) to the other coder to apply the method. The second approach is for the coders to conduct the word association contextualization steps described in this chapter independently using Mozdeh to generate random samples rather than sharing saved documents.

Whichever approach is used, the results should be compared only after the coders have completed the task. Disagreements should be resolved through discussion.

4.6 REPORTING WAA

WAA without a follow-up thematic analysis is suitable when the WAD stage identifies a small set of words to analyze so that it is not necessary to group the words into themes. For example, if only 1–25 words are identified, then they might all be reported separately. When there are too many words to report individually, a thematic analysis stage should be applied to group words into a smaller number of themes to report. Since there will normally be fewer than 25 words for a WAA, they can be reported in a table or bullet point list, stating the word as well as a description of its meaning and context within the dataset. If relevant, the frequency of the words in the datasets could also be reported (e.g., % of female % of male and % of nonbinary texts containing the term). Alternatively, if extensive discussions are needed about the contexts of the terms, then separate paragraphs could be used instead of a table or bullet point list.

An academic paper or dissertation usually discusses results rather than just reporting them. This discussion could be placed in a separate Discussion section after the results (e.g., especially if relating the results to existing published research) or could appear alongside the results in the same section (e.g., especially for analytic discussions not relying on existing published research).

4.7 SUMMARY

The word association detection of the previous chapter produces a list of words that occur disproportionately often in one subset than another. For example, if the two sets are tweets by males and females then WAD words would be more used by one of these two genders. The methods in this chapter disambiguate the words to identify their most common meaning in the two sets (in case they are polysemic or used within common phrases) and identifies their typical context so that general inferences can be drawn from each term. Together the two methods comprise word association analysis:

$$WAA = WAD + WAC.$$

The primary WAC method is to read a sample of texts containing the term to identify the main meaning and context. If this fails, two advanced types of follow-up word association tests can be used. The first is general, using WAD to find words in the complete corpus of texts that associate with the term, allowing patterns to be found in the words used alongside it in texts. As with the random sample method, this attempts to identify a common overall meaning or context. In contrast, the second follow-up WAD method is based on the assumption that the term is used in multiple different contexts, but that at least one of these contexts is more common in one subset than the other. If all three of these methods fail, then the creative thinking approach can be tried. It will help to systematically record the results in a table to keep track of them (Table 4.7).

Table 4.7: A table to track the meaning and context of a word association analysis of terms used more by males than females in a set of Covid-19 tweets. Creative thinking is needed when none work, as in the final example

Term	Meaning	Context	Random	Term WAA	Subset WAA
Trump	Donald Trump	Covid-19 pronouncements	95% of 20 tweets	-	-
5G	5G	Cause of Covid-19 symptoms	Unclear	Cause (29%)	-
ppl	people	Politics and economics	Unclear	Unclear	@pmoindia, trade
It	Pronoun	Information (creative method)	Unclear	Unclear	Unclear

The final check needed when reporting the results is for the cause of the word association: spam/bots, dates, news stories, viral sharing, societal changes, or something else. This information is needed to make inferences about the word associations found.

CHAPTER 5

Word Association Thematic Analysis: Theme Detection

A word association analysis (WAA) with too many significant terms to list individually (e.g., more than 15–25) needs a method to group the words together for reporting. Detailing long lists of significant terms is undesirable because they would be difficult for the reader to digest. Moreover, the information conveyed by the terms may overlap or could be better understood when these connections are explicit. This is achieved in this chapter with a thematic analysis of the WAA terms (Figure 1.1). The thematic analysis (TA) groups together related terms so that a small set of coherent themes can be reported instead of a long list of terms. The grouping exercise can also help with interpreting the individual terms by providing additional perspectives on them.

Word association thematic analysis (WATA) is a variant of the standard qualitative research method of reflexive thematic analysis (Braun and Clarke, 2006, 2013; see also: www.psych.auckland.ac.nz/en/about/thematic-analysis.html), where the objects to be organized thematically are contextualized words rather than codes applied to texts. The core idea behind thematic analysis is to identify themes by annotating texts (words in this case) with ideas for themes, then organize the initial ideas into coherent themes by repeated re-reading and grouping similar themes. Thematic analysis is a flexible technique, but this chapter recommends a default way of applying it after WAA.

5.1 ASSIGNING THEMES TO WORDS

The thematic analysis part of WATA involves assigning themes to the contextualized words from the WAC list (Step 3 below). While the WAC stage attributes a meaning and context to each word in the WAD list, a theme *generalizes* the WAC context to help group together related terms. A theme is a generalization, where the texts containing the words are expressions of the theme. The theme does not have to encapsulate the meaning and context of the word in entirety, but it should be clear that there is a good fit between the word and the theme. Themes can only be identified after the WAC step is complete for all words because creating a new theme involves identifying similarities between multiple words, and differences from other words in the set, so that they could fit a single theme. Thus, identifying a theme is a type of clustering: grouping words together under a single generalizing description. Other approaches to identify themes can be tried if this method does not work (Ryan and Bernard, 2003).

To illustrate the process of theme generation, suppose that a project has the research question: What types of popular culture are discussed differently on Twitter by UK and U.S. visitors to Ibiza? Suppose also that tweeting about social events in Ibiza found the words shown in Table 5.1 to be used more by UK-based than U.S.-based tweeters. Two themes have been assigned to the words. One theme is relatively straightforward: Social dance style is appropriate as a clear generalization of three different named dance styles. The other theme, Dance venue, fits *Warehouse* and *Amnesia* well and is also a reasonable fit for *DJ* and *Bar*, since these are important components of most dance venues.

Table 5.1: Words, contexts, and themes for a set of popular culture related tweets

Word	Meaning and context	Theme
Melbourne	Melbourne shuffle dance	Social dance style
DJ	Dance event DJ	Dance venue
Amnesia	Ibiza dance club Amnesia	Dance venue
Hakken	Hakken rave dance	Social dance style
Gloving	Glove-using dance	Social dance style
Warehouse	Warehouse to host rave	Dance venue
Bar	Bar in dance club	Dance venue

Themes relevant to the research goals are likely to be most useful, but others can be used if necessary. The themes might be informed by prior theory or knowledge, if relevant, but care should be taken with any pre-existing themes to ensure that they fit well with the WAC results.

5.2 WATA PROCEDURE

This section introduces the steps of the TA stage of WATA, adding them to the WAA steps. The steps organize all or part of the word association analysis word list, depending on the length of the list.

1. Conduct WAD and select the 100 most statistically significant terms from the WAA list (with at least one star), or the complete list if there are less than 100–200.

2. Apply WAC to the selected terms.

3. For each word in the list, add a theme that generalizes its context (if possible) in a way that may be helpful to the research goals. Multiple themes can be added if relevant.

4. Read through the word list again, comparing the themes and merging similar ones. If necessary, return to the WAC stage to check whether a theme fits. The themes produced by this stage are the narrow themes.

5. If many themes (more than 15) have been identified by stage 4 then group these narrow themes into related sets of broad themes, repeatedly comparing broad themes, and returning to the previous stage if necessary.

6. Select the *next* 20 most statistically significant terms (if any), detect their contexts (Step 2) and either assign them narrow or broad themes so that they fit into the existing groups or create new narrow and/or broad themes if necessary. When new themes are created, check if existing terms may fit into them.

7. Stop when theme saturation has been reached in the sense that a set of 20 terms has not produced a new narrow theme or a substantial new perspective on the existing themes.

8. Name and define the themes detected.

9. Write up the results with paraphrased examples of the terms used in context. Paraphrasing is normally required for ethical reasons: to preserve the anonymity of the users.

The heart of this method is the combination of assigning themes to words, grouping themes together, and constant comparison to ensure consistency of the themes across the whole set of words. A major difference from a standard reflexive thematic analysis is that the initial stage above of term meaning and context detection (WAA) replaces the usual "familiarization with the data" first stage of TA, involving reading all texts to be thematically analyzed. All WATAs so far have used inductive TA—deducing the themes from the text rather than based on prior theory—but other forms are also possible.

While the above method provides a simple criterion for identifying a type of theme saturation, in practice the decision about when to stop analyzing new words may also be influenced by the research questions or goals, the type of data, and the confidence of the coders in the theme generation process. The issue of when to stop thematic analysis studies has many different perspectives, often centring on the concept of data saturation (Guest, Namey, and Chen, 2020). Nevertheless, since in reflexive thematic analysis, "meaning is generated through interpretation of, not excavated from, data" (Braun and Clarke, 2019), rigid rules are inappropriate, including advance specification of the number of texts to read. The above guidelines for when to stop analyzing new should therefore be overridden when judged necessary.

5.3 WATA VISUAL AND PERFORMING ARTS EXAMPLE

This example investigates gender differences in the academic articles written by men and women about visual and performing arts. The data consists of the articles, titles, and keywords of 48,890 visual and performing arts articles published between 1996 and 2019. This example illustrates how WATA can be applied to these texts to discover gender differences themes. The spreadsheet produced can be found online at: https://doi.org/10.6084/m9.figshare.12884798. The following actions were used for this project.

- The abstracts of visual and performing arts articles were downloaded from an academic database and imported into Mozdeh using the Import Data button.
- WAD was applied in Mozdeh by selecting the Association Mining Comparisons tab, checking the *Compare Male v Female for each query* option and then clicking the *Compare words matching the above queries button* (with a blank query box). This produced a list of words associated with female or male authors of visual and performing arts articles. This text file was loaded into Excel for convenience (Figure 5.1). It can be seen, for example, that the term "women" was in 1.5% of male texts but 7.0% of female texts, with this difference being highly statistically significant (three stars) despite being small (5.4% after rounding).
- A female filter was set in Mozdeh, the Save tab selected and the WATA button clicked, selecting the results file and accepting the option to use the current search filters to produce a list of texts matching each word. This was loaded into a separate tab in Excel (Figure 5.2). This was repeated for males.

The above steps produced an Excel spreadsheet with a list of gendered terms in one worksheet and a random sample of articles using those terms for each gender in two further worksheets. This information was used for a WATA, as follows.

For the word association detection stage of WATA, each word in the list with three stars (very strongly statistically significant gender difference) was checked for meaning and context by reading a sample of at least ten texts containing it from the relevant worksheet, then assigning it a word association context. The contexts have been added to the final column of the worksheet. The context description should encapsulate the main uses of the term in the context of this data set. Here are some examples to illustrate the decision-making process.

- The term "dance" has many different possible contexts, including individual types of dance (e.g., ballet, contemporary, disco, hip hop), theater/concert dance, social dance, and electronic dance music. The term could also be used about learning to dance, dance compositions, or dance performances. Reading a sample of texts containing the term

(Figure 5.2), suggests that the appropriate context is *theater dance*. Almost all the texts seem to be about learning or critiquing theatrical dance performances.

- The term "women" seemed to be used in a wide variety of different contexts so no way could be found to narrow it down further. Someone with more expert knowledge reading the texts matching "women" in the online data might find a narrower context, however.

- The term "her" referred to women in different contexts, but they were always academic authors, artists (e.g., playwrights) or the author herself. A theme was chosen reflecting these contexts after some thought (the initial theme was "women" but it was changed after realizing that "men" was not appropriate for "he").

- The term "he" referred to men in different contexts, but they were always academic authors, artists (e.g., playwrights) or other cultural figures, such as art exhibition curators. The men were only rarely abstract, such as theater audience members. For example, in "from the moment he arrived in Cuenca **he** demonstrated particular interest in the cloister," the term "he" refers to Bishop Quiroga and the article discusses his relationship to the cloister of Cuenca Cathedral. The context of "he" differs somewhat from the context of "she," which was not used often to refer to culturally important figures but was instead often used to refer to the article author.

- The term "explore" was typically used to describe what the author did, so is related to their methods and was given word association context *Exploratory methods*.

- I could not find a common theme for the term "their" other than the fact that it almost always referred to people.

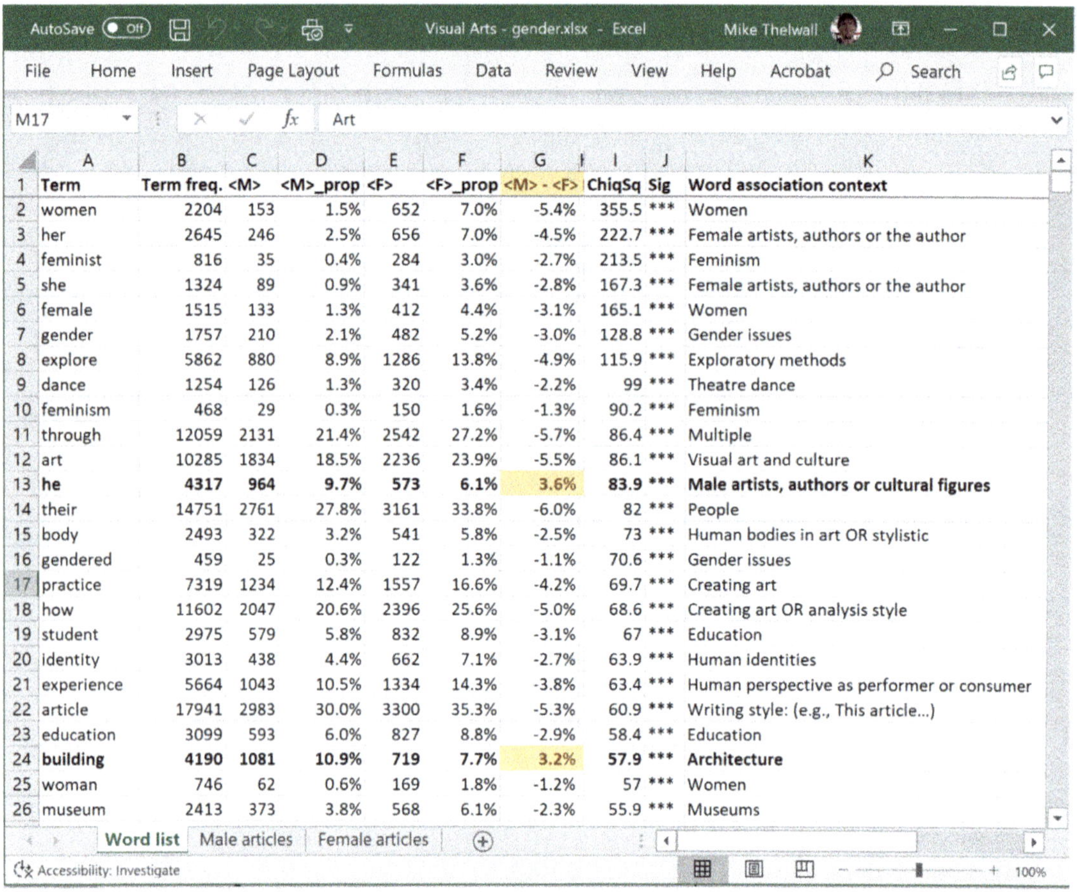

Term	Term freq.	<M>	<M>_prop	<F>	<F>_prop	<M> - <F>	ChiqSq	Sig	Word association context
women	2204	153	1.5%	652	7.0%	-5.4%	355.5	***	Women
her	2645	246	2.5%	656	7.0%	-4.5%	222.7	***	Female artists, authors or the author
feminist	816	35	0.4%	284	3.0%	-2.7%	213.5	***	Feminism
she	1324	89	0.9%	341	3.6%	-2.8%	167.3	***	Female artists, authors or the author
female	1515	133	1.3%	412	4.4%	-3.1%	165.1	***	Women
gender	1757	210	2.1%	482	5.2%	-3.0%	128.8	***	Gender issues
explore	5862	880	8.9%	1286	13.8%	-4.9%	115.9	***	Exploratory methods
dance	1254	126	1.3%	320	3.4%	-2.2%	99	***	Theatre dance
feminism	468	29	0.3%	150	1.6%	-1.3%	90.2	***	Feminism
through	12059	2131	21.4%	2542	27.2%	-5.7%	86.4	***	Multiple
art	10285	1834	18.5%	2236	23.9%	-5.5%	86.1	***	Visual art and culture
he	**4317**	**964**	**9.7%**	**573**	**6.1%**	**3.6%**	**83.9**	*******	**Male artists, authors or cultural figures**
their	14751	2761	27.8%	3161	33.8%	-6.0%	82	***	People
body	2493	322	3.2%	541	5.8%	-2.5%	73	***	Human bodies in art OR stylistic
gendered	459	25	0.3%	122	1.3%	-1.1%	70.6	***	Gender issues
practice	7319	1234	12.4%	1557	16.6%	-4.2%	69.7	***	Creating art
how	11602	2047	20.6%	2396	25.6%	-5.0%	68.6	***	Creating art OR analysis style
student	2975	579	5.8%	832	8.9%	-3.1%	67	***	Education
identity	3013	438	4.4%	662	7.1%	-2.7%	63.9	***	Human identities
experience	5664	1043	10.5%	1334	14.3%	-3.8%	63.4	***	Human perspective as performer or consumer
article	17941	2983	30.0%	3300	35.3%	-5.3%	60.9	***	Writing style: (e.g., This article...)
education	3099	593	6.0%	827	8.8%	-2.9%	58.4	***	Education
building	**4190**	**1081**	**10.9%**	**719**	**7.7%**	**3.2%**	**57.9**	*******	**Architecture**
woman	746	62	0.6%	169	1.8%	-1.2%	57	***	Women
museum	2413	373	3.8%	568	6.1%	-2.3%	55.9	***	Museums

Figure 5.1: Gendered words from the articles, titles, and keywords of a set of 48,890 visual and performing arts articles published between 1996 and 2019, as identified by Mozdeh. Male results are bold. This spreadsheet is online: https://doi.org/10.6084/m9.figshare.12884798.

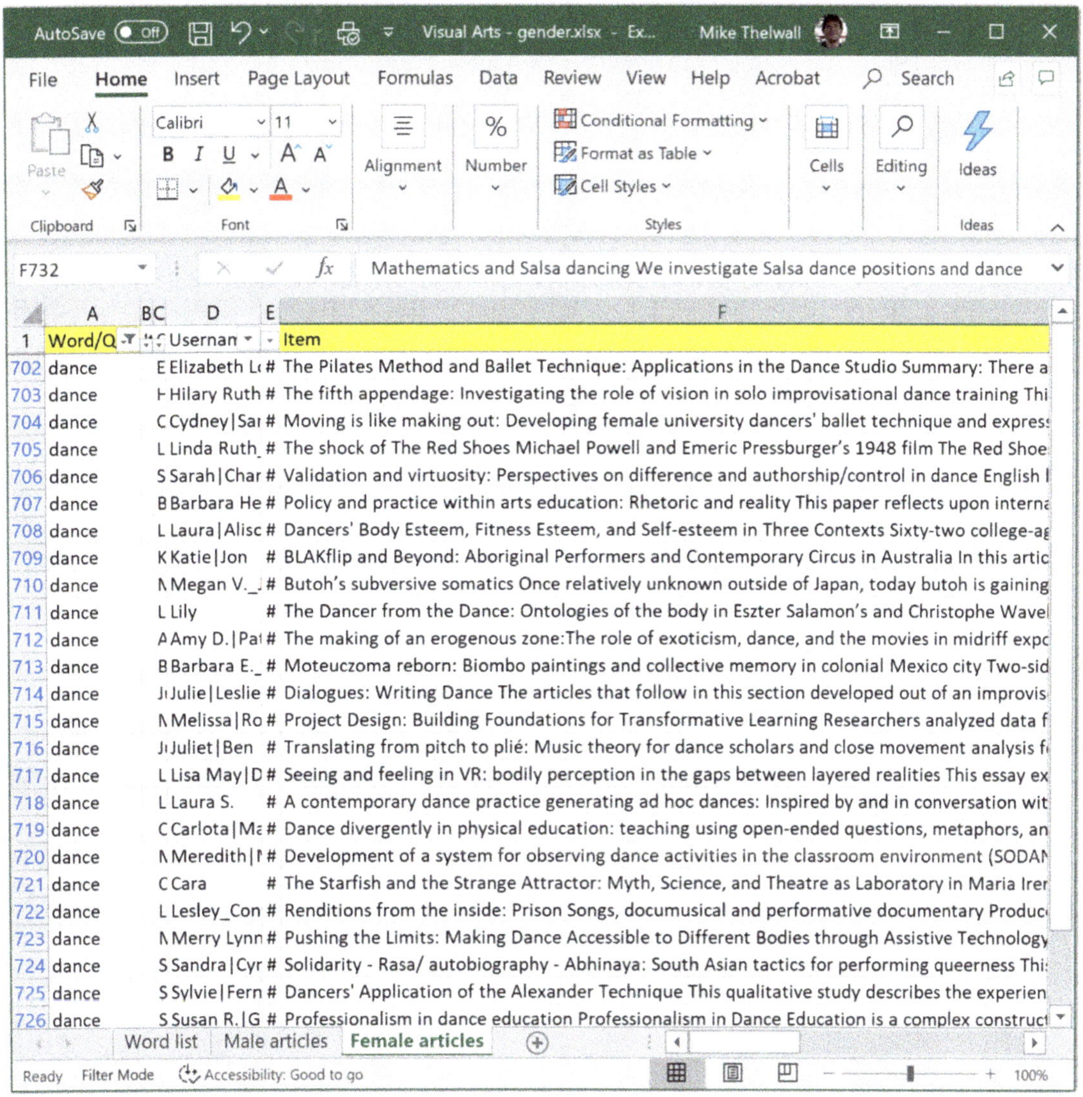

Figure 5.2: Random female-authored visual and performing arts articles containing the term "dance", as identified by the WATA button in Mozdeh. This spreadsheet is online: https://doi.org/10.6084/m9.figshare.12884798.

The narrow thematic analysis stage may reuse the WAC descriptions or generalize them if this helps to cover multiple terms. Thus, the relatively specific word association contexts may be relaxed to fit in with others into a single theme. For example, two slightly different male and female word association contexts for she/he were changed to *Individual women/men* since the difference did not seem to be important (a subjective judgment) (Figure 5.3). This could be considered if the initial allocation of themes gives too many to report or obscures trends in the results. This stage might correct mistakes identified in the earlier stage, such as changing *Human bodies in art* to *Multiple* (Figure 5.3).

If there are many narrow themes, then it can help to group them into broad themes to aid with reporting (Figure 5.3). These do not usually replace the original themes but may help to organize the themes.

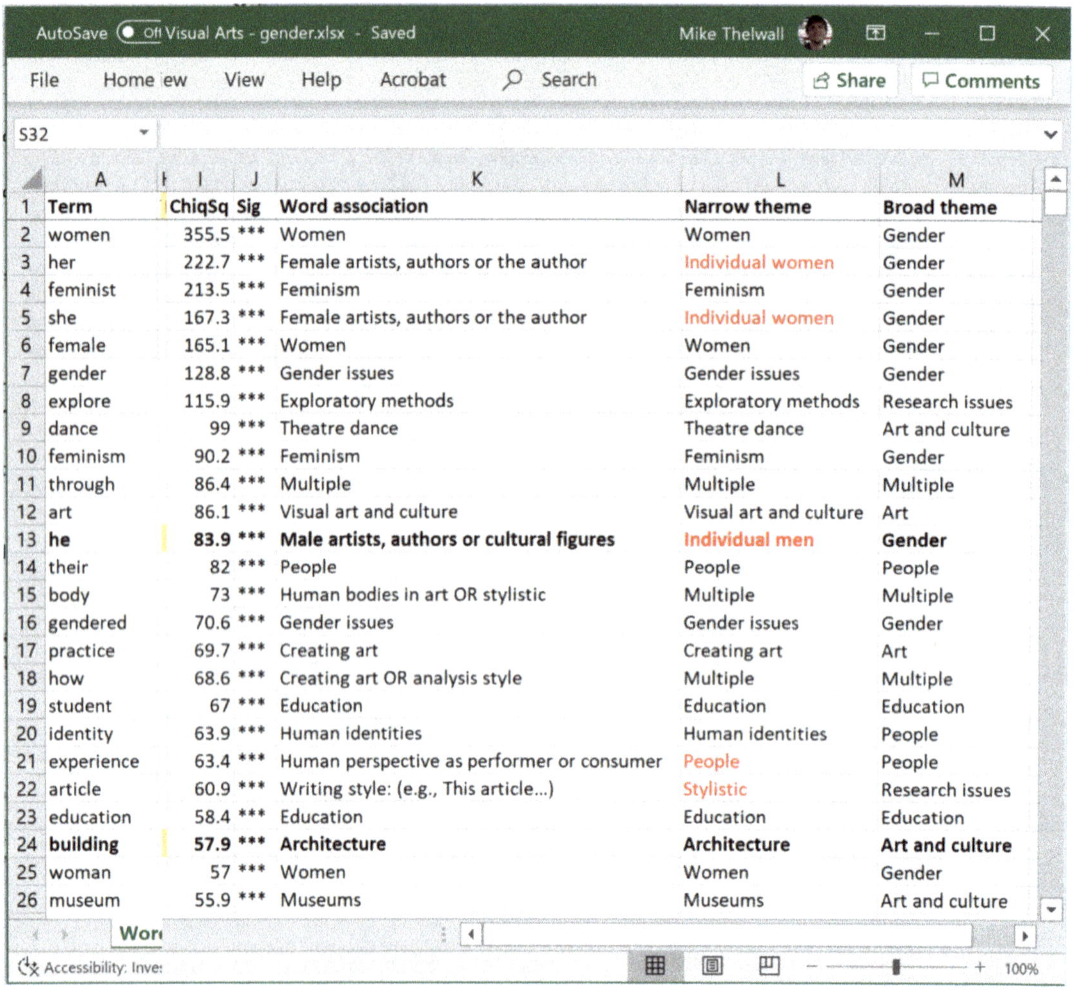

	A	I	J	K	L	M
1	**Term**	**ChiqSq**	**Sig**	**Word association**	**Narrow theme**	**Broad theme**
2	women	355.5	***	Women	Women	Gender
3	her	222.7	***	Female artists, authors or the author	Individual women	Gender
4	feminist	213.5	***	Feminism	Feminism	Gender
5	she	167.3	***	Female artists, authors or the author	Individual women	Gender
6	female	165.1	***	Women	Women	Gender
7	gender	128.8	***	Gender issues	Gender issues	Gender
8	explore	115.9	***	Exploratory methods	Exploratory methods	Research issues
9	dance	99	***	Theatre dance	Theatre dance	Art and culture
10	feminism	90.2	***	Feminism	Feminism	Gender
11	through	86.4	***	Multiple	Multiple	Multiple
12	art	86.1	***	Visual art and culture	Visual art and culture	Art
13	**he**	**83.9**	***	**Male artists, authors or cultural figures**	**Individual men**	**Gender**
14	their	82	***	People	People	People
15	body	73	***	Human bodies in art OR stylistic	Multiple	Multiple
16	gendered	70.6	***	Gender issues	Gender issues	Gender
17	practice	69.7	***	Creating art	Creating art	Art
18	how	68.6	***	Creating art OR analysis style	Multiple	Multiple
19	student	67	***	Education	Education	Education
20	identity	63.9	***	Human identities	Human identities	People
21	experience	63.4	***	Human perspective as performer or consumer	People	People
22	article	60.9	***	Writing style: (e.g., This article...)	Stylistic	Research issues
23	education	58.4	***	Education	Education	Education
24	**building**	**57.9**	***	**Architecture**	**Architecture**	**Art and culture**
25	woman	57	***	Women	Women	Gender
26	museum	55.9	***	Museums	Museums	Art and culture

Figure 5.3: Word associations, narrow themes, and broad themes from the visual and performing arts dataset. Red indicates theme changes from word associations. This spreadsheet is online: https://doi.org/10.6084/m9.figshare.12884798.

5.4 USING MULTIPLE CODERS

WATA is subjective and can therefore benefit from employing multiple coders, comparing the results and producing a consensus. This improves the trustworthiness of the results by ensuring that they do not reflect a single person's uncritical perspective (for general reporting guidelines, see also O'Brien, et al., 2014). Inter-coder consistency scores, as used in content analysis (Neuendorf, 2016), are not appropriate for thematic analysis, but could be used for a follow-up content analysis of the TA themes, if necessary. Additional coders are particularly important when the meaning of the texts may not be transparent, including when there is a likelihood of sarcasm, figurative language, sublanguage terms, or hidden meanings. Multiple coders are necessary for the TA stage of WATA and the WAC stage of WAA, but not for the WAC stage of WATA because the TA component subsumes the WAC results. If there are major problems of disagreement in the TA results, then the WAC stage could be revisited by both TA coders.

For the thematic analysis component, each coder should independently apply the thematic stages in the subsection above, then compare and discuss their themes. The final set of themes should be achieved through discussion with the goal of generating a list of themes that accurately reflect the data and are relevant to the research aims. One coder can apply the WAC stage and pass the results to the other coder, with both applying TA to the WAC results. Alternatively, both might apply both stages, but only compare the TA results.

5.5 REPORTING WATA

WATA results can be reported in a table, graph, bullet point list, or series of paragraphs. These variations are illustrated in the cited references and the examples chapter. Each row/bullet point/paragraph should report the theme name, a theme definition or contextual information, and a list of words within the theme. These words can include the percentages of matching texts containing the term and the percentage of non-matching texts containing it. If there are too many words to report, then a sample could be given instead. Many WATA studies have not reported theme descriptions because the word lists serve to clarify the meaning of the theme name, but it would be clearer to include a description as well as the list of WAD terms.

Although WATA is ultimately a qualitative method and the bullet point or paragraphs methods for reporting the results may fit best with the qualitative approach, tables help the reader to understand what the core results are. The nature of the results can otherwise be confusing because of the multiple stages needed for a WATA. Including percentages for the matching and non-matching terms (e.g., "omg" was in 5% of female-authored tweets compared to 2% of male-authored tweets) is useful to help the reader to set the results in the context of the data.

5.5.1 THEME PREVALENCE INFORMATION

Evidence about the prevalence of a theme in the data would be more useful to report than the prevalence of the WAD words within the theme. The WATA method does not give direct evidence of the overall prevalence of a theme, however. This contrasts with content analysis, which gives estimates about the percentage of texts matching its categories. Since WATA is based on words and a theme could be discussed using words not found in the WAD stage, WATA can only give estimates of the minimum extent to which a theme is discussed.

Three stages are needed to obtain minimum theme discussion evidence for each theme because the calculation needs to combine data from all words within the theme, as follows.

1. For each WAD word, multiply the prevalence of the word in the reported set (e.g., females, U.S.-authored) by the percentage of texts about the theme in the WAC sample. For instance, suppose that one of the female-associated WAD words within the WATA Support theme for a gender-based WATA was *helping*, which was in 20% of female-authored tweets. Suppose also that 90% of the WAC sample of female-authored tweets containing *helping* had a context of support/helping, fitting within the WATA Support theme. Combining these, 90% × 20% = 18% of female-authored tweets contain the word *helping* with a context fitting within the Support WATA theme.

2. Total the estimated theme prevalence percentages for each WAD word within the theme. For example, suppose the Support theme for female-authored tweets included three WAD terms: *care*, *support*, and *helping*. Suppose also the step 1 calculation for these words gave WATA support theme prevalence estimates as follows: *care*: 10%; *support*: 12%; *helping*: 18%. Then the initial WATA minimum prevalence estimate would be the sum of these: 10% + 12% +1 8% = 40%. The initial estimate is therefore that 40% of female-authored tweets discuss the Support WATA theme.

3. The initial estimate from the step above overlooks that texts may contain multiple WAD terms, so a correction step is needed to account for this. This correction step uses the percentage overlap between the categories. For this, count the number of texts containing each term separately (e.g., Mozdeh reports this when the term is entered as a query) and the number of texts containing any of the terms (e.g., in Mozdeh enter all terms together in the search). Dividing the latter by the former gives a correction factor to multiply the initial prevalence figure by. For example, suppose that the number of female-authored texts containing the 3 words above is: *care*: 1,000; *helping*: 2,000; *support*: 3,000. Suppose also that the query *care helping support* identifies that 4,000 female-authored texts contain any one of the 3 terms. Then the

correction factor is 4,000/(1,000 + 2,000 + 3,000), which is 80%. Thus, the initial prevalence estimate of 40% needs to be corrected by multiplying by 80% to give a corrected estimate. In summary, at least 40% × 80% = 32% of female-authored tweets discuss the Support WATA theme, according to this estimate.

After repeating the above steps, the prevalence information can be added to a table summarizing the themes found (e.g., Table 5.2). The prevalence information here gives an indication of which are numerically the most important themes.

The above steps can be repeated for the comparator set (male and nonbinary-authored tweets in the above example) using the prevalence percentages for the comparator set found by the WAD stage. Although the prevalence percentages for individual words were calculated from the matching set (female-authored texts in the above example) in the WAA stage, it seems reasonable to use these same percentages for the comparator set. For example, suppose that the male and non-binary percentage for the word *helping* was 15%. Then using the above-mentioned estimate that 90% of *helping* words (for females) are used in the context of support/helping, this would give an estimate of 15% × 90% = 14% of male and non-binary *helping* words being used in the context of support/helping. Suppose that similar calculations for *support* gave 9% and for *care* gave 6%, giving an initial prevalence estimate of 14% + 9% + 6% = 29%. Suppose also that the number of male and nonbinary-authored texts containing the three words above is: *care*: 1,000; *helping*: 1,000; *support*: 2,000. The query *care helping support* identifies that 3,000 male and nonbinary-authored texts contain any one of the three terms. Then the correction factor is 3,000/(1,000 + 1,000 + 2,000), which is 75%. Thus, the initial prevalence estimate of 29% needs to be corrected by multiplying by 75% to give a corrected estimate. After this, at least 29% × 75% = 22% of male and nonbinary-authored tweets discuss the Support WATA theme, according to this estimate.

Table 5.2: Examples of WATA themes found for female-authored tweets compared to male and nonbinary-authored tweets within an illness-related Covid-19 collection. The theme column also includes an estimate of the minimum prevalence of the theme within female-authored tweets compared to male and nonbinary-authored tweets. This table illustrates how themes might be reported

Theme	Theme description	Terms in theme: female% v. others%
Support (32% vs. 24%)	Helping or support for others during Covid-19 restrictions.	*care*: 10% vs. 6%; *support*: 12% vs. 9%; *helping*: 18% vs. 14%
Hospital (8% vs. 5%)	Hospital visits or the need to hospitalize victims.	Hospital: 6% vs. 4%; *ambulance*: 2% vs. 1%; *emergency*: 3% vs. 1%
Protection (5% vs. 2%)	Ensuring an infected person does not spread Covid-19.	*isolate*: 3% vs. 1%; *mask*: 2% vs. 1%; *separate*: 2% vs. 1%.

5.5.2 DISCUSSING THE RESULTS

The results can be discussed in the section reporting them (especially if also analyzing them) or in a follow-up Discussion section (especially if relating the results to prior published research papers). Care should be taken to avoid claiming that the study has found statistical evidence for the themes overall because the statistical evidence is only for the individual terms within the theme and not the theme overall.

5.6 SUMMARY

A word association thematic analysis is produced by starting from a word association analysis and then applying thematic analysis (TA) to organize the words into themes:

WATA = WAA + TA

The purpose of WATA is to cope with the situation when a WAA produces too many terms to report individually and some of the terms are related. The thematic part involves starting by assigning the words to potentially relevant themes, then going through an iterative process of grouping, merging, and comparing the tags until a coherent stable set of themes emerges. This set of themes can then be reported as the main outcome of the analysis. A study may conduct a single WATA or, if using the subset A vs. subset B approach, may conduct two WATAs, one for each subset (Figure 5.4). In this case, the two WATAs should be conducted separately because it is likely that the themes will not overlap at all.

Although the WAC and TA stages are conceptually separate, they can be conducted partly simultaneously: annotating terms with initial theme ideas after detecting their contexts. This is useful for efficiency and helps to focus the coder's mind on the difference between the two steps. The next chapter summarizes a set of WATA studies, illustrating a range of ways in which the method can be applied.

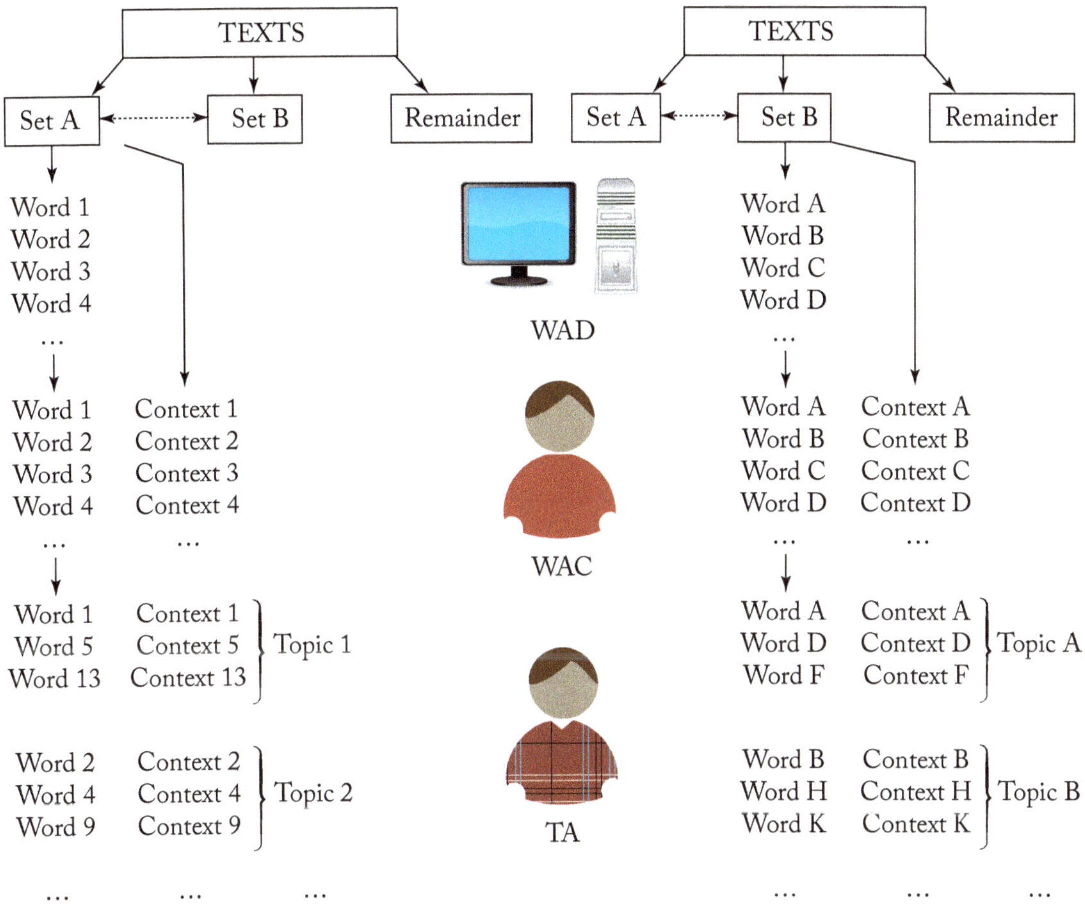

Figure 5.4: The steps for two separate WATAs on the same set of texts, one conducted for each subset.

CHAPTER 6

Word Association Thematic Analysis Examples

This chapter reports a series of different types of WATA, focusing on the results and data sources and picking out a few methods details. Each is based on a published journal article with an open access version online.

6.1 GENDER DIFFERENCES IN EARLY COVID-19 TWEETING

WATA has been used to find gender differences in tweeting in English about Covid-19 when some countries were entering lockdown phases, March 10–23, 2020 (Thelwall and Thelwall, 2020). Mozdeh was used to collect tweets with a set of relevant queries (coronavirus; "corona virus"; Covid-19; Covid19) and then WATA was applied, with 103 gendered terms detected. The WAD component was modified to adjust for the news-driven nature of the issue. The modification involved applying WAD to each day separately (rather than the whole period in one go), focusing on terms that had gained at least at least 7 statistical significance stars for daily gender differences over the 14 days. This step filtered out many terms related to news stories that were discussed only briefly.

WAC was relatively straightforward in some cases. For example, "football" was used in tweets discussing the cancellation of football matches or the suspension of the (U.S. or UK, American football or soccer) football season. The term "game" was usually used in the context of sports game cancellations rather than computer games, as was evident from reading a random sample of tweets. The term "@pmoindia" and similar terms seemed to be primarily used (presumably by Indians) to tweet requests directly to the Prime Minister of India, which was a surprising inclusion given that nothing similar was seen for the U.S. president (U.S. requests were more gender balanced).

The thematic analysis produced ten narrow themes, some male (Figures 6.1–6.4), some female (Figures 6.5–6.8) and some mixed (Figures 6.9 and 6.10). For example, males seemed to be more interested in tweeting about sport than were females, and females were more likely to tweet about social distancing. A separate graph was produced for each theme to emphasize that each word within the theme might be important.

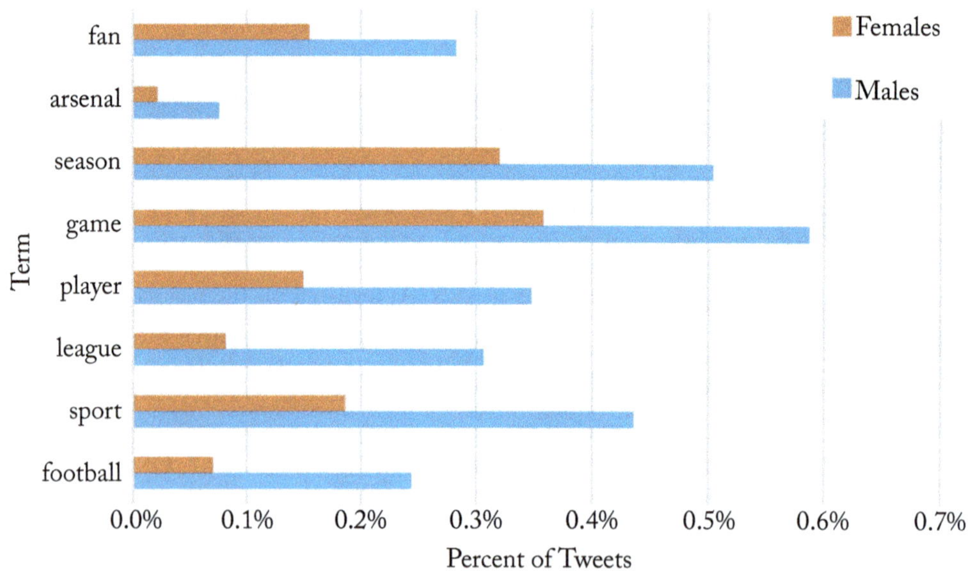

Figure 6.1: Male Covid-19 theme: Sport-related terms with statistically significant gender differences in usage (Thelwall and Thelwall, 2020).

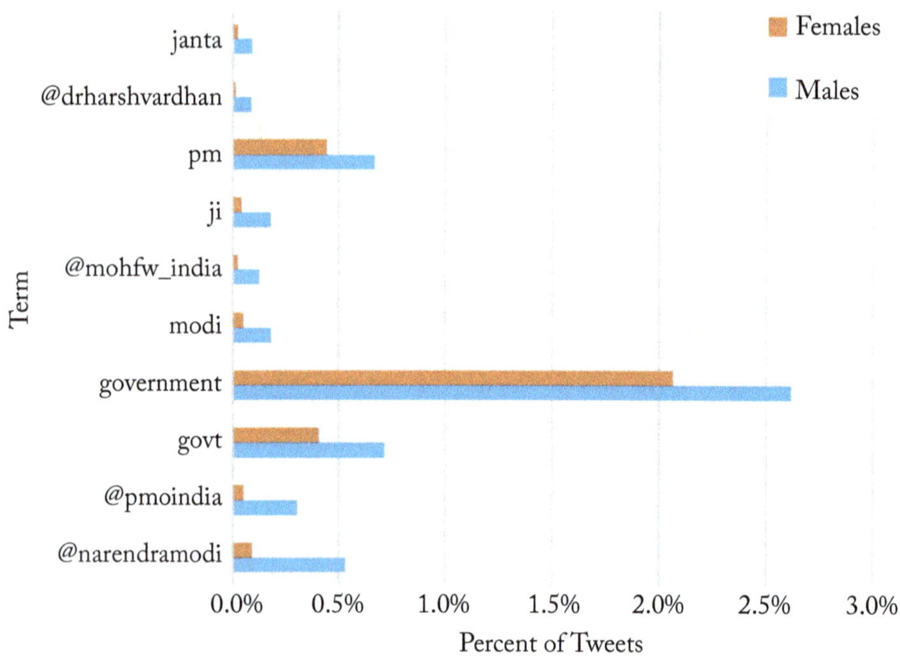

Figure 6.2: Male Covid-19 theme: Politics-related terms with statistically significant gender differences in usage (Thelwall and Thelwall, 2020).

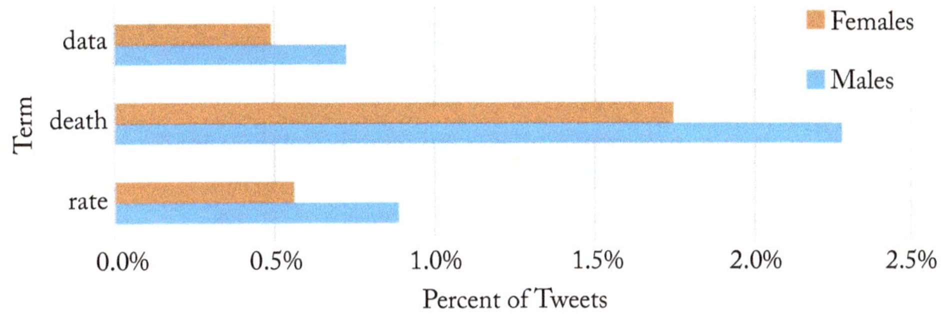

Figure 6.3: Male Covid-19 theme: Epidemiology-related terms with statistically significant gender differences in usage (Thelwall and Thelwall, 2020).

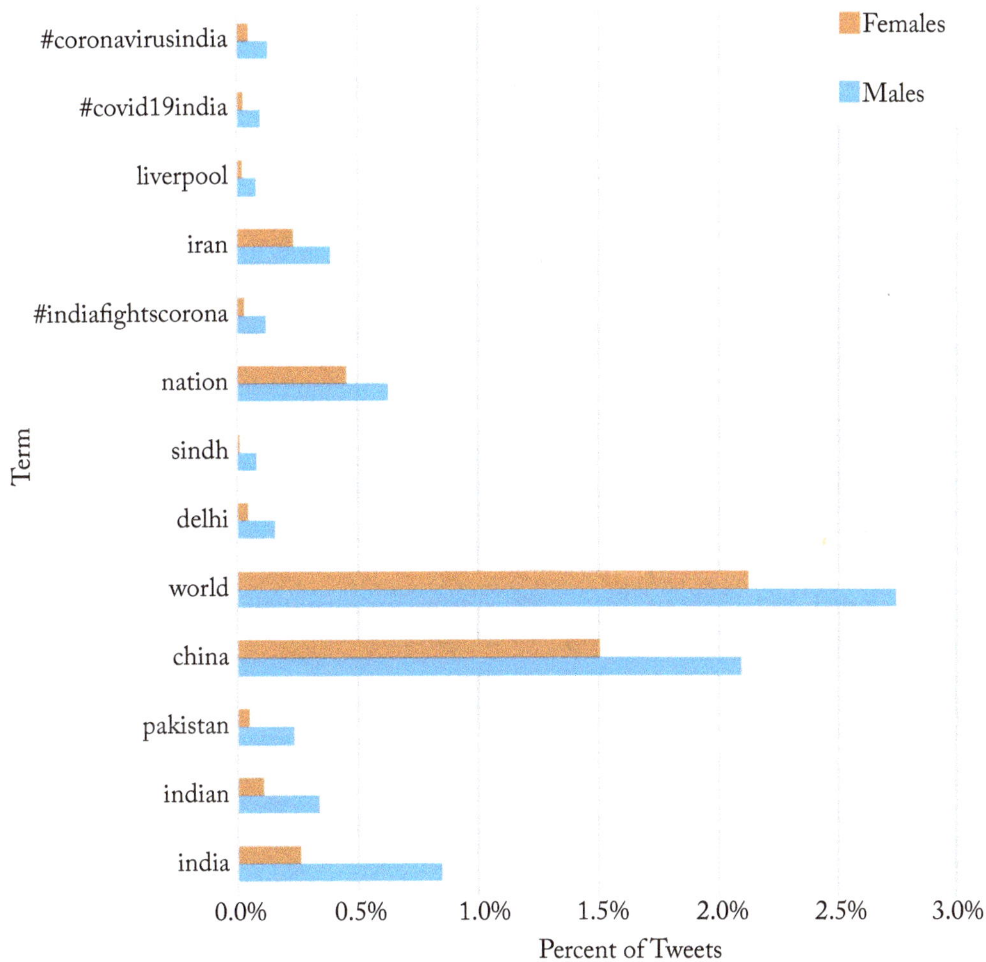

Figure 6.4: Male Covid-19 theme: Geography-related terms with statistically significant gender differences in usage (Liverpool is also sport-related) (Thelwall and Thelwall, 2020).

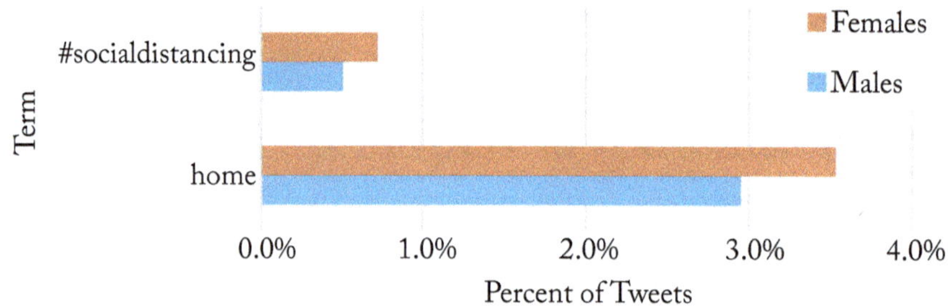

Figure 6.5: Female Covid-19 theme: Social distancing-related terms with statistically significant gender differences in usage (Thelwall and Thelwall, 2020).

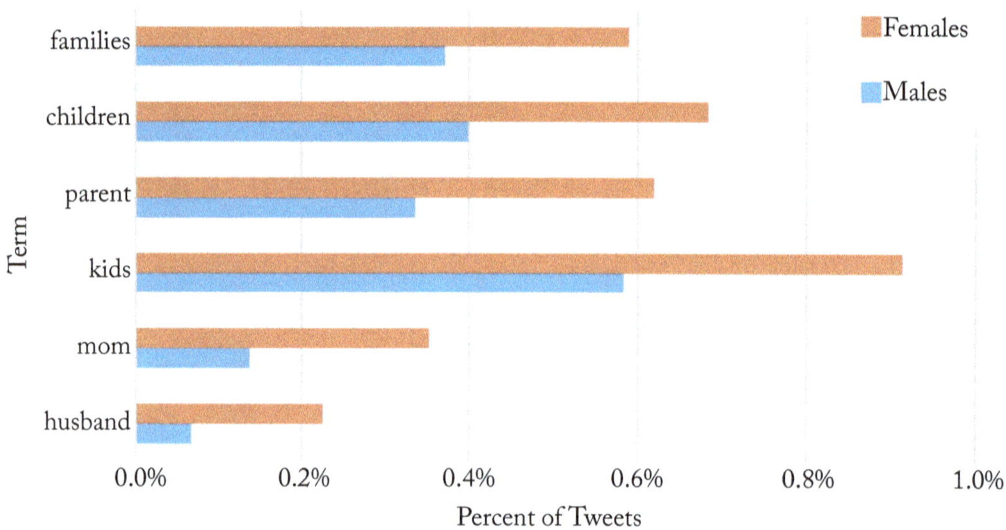

Figure 6.6: Female Covid-19 theme: Family-related terms with statistically significant gender differences in usage (Thelwall and Thelwall, 2020).

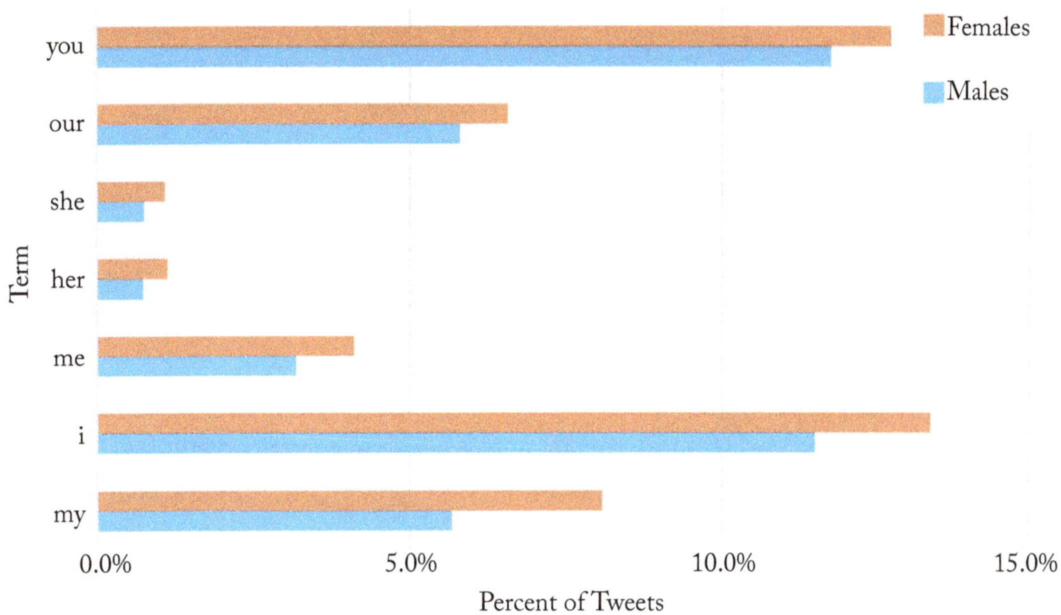

Figure 6.7: Female Covid-19 theme: Pronouns with statistically significant gender differences in usage (Thelwall and Thelwall, 2020).

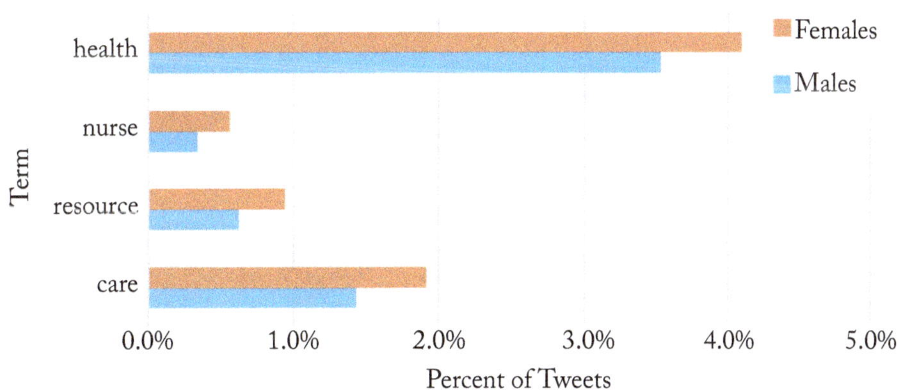

Figure 6.8: Female Covid-19 theme: Healthcare-related terms with statistically significant gender differences in usage (Thelwall and Thelwall, 2020).

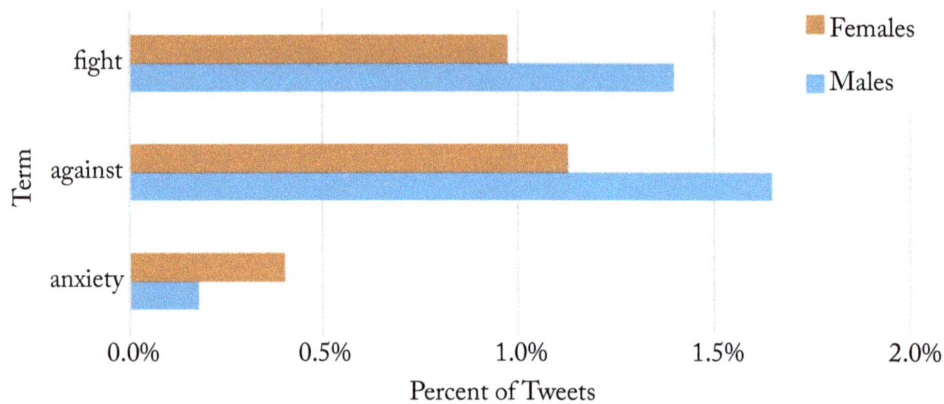

Figure 6.9: Mixed-gender Covid-19 theme: Fight or worry-related terms with statistically significant gender differences in usage (Thelwall and Thelwall, 2020).

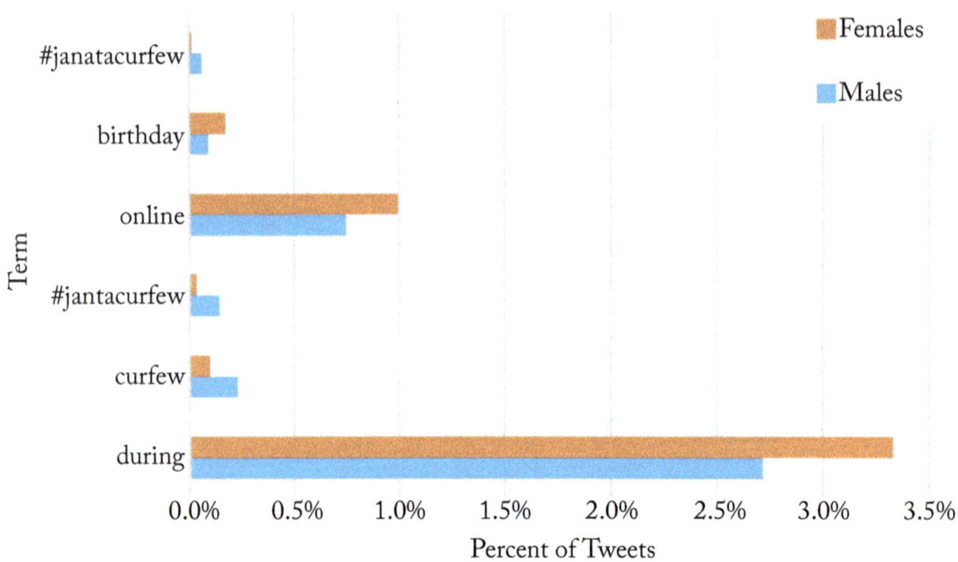

Figure 6.10: Mixed-gender Covid-19 theme: Curfew-related terms with statistically significant gender differences in usage (Thelwall and Thelwall, 2020).

6.2 GENDER DIFFERENCES IN MUSEUM COMMENTS ON YOUTUBE

Gender differences in online reactions to museums have been investigated by harvesting comments from the videos in 50 large museum YouTube channels based in English-speaking nations (Thelwall, 2018c). Mozdeh was used to harvest the comments on all videos from the channels and WATA used to identify the core-gendered themes (Tables 6.1, 6.2).

For the WAC stage, some words were unambiguous (e.g., *bra*) but others had contexts that were only evident from reading random samples of YouTube comments containing them. For example, while *Corey* is a first name, in this context it referred to a painting instructor. Similarly, while *bat* could mean baseball or cricket bat, in the museum comments it usually meant the bats in a Smithsonian video about vampire bats sucking blood.

The thematic analysis in this case produced highly varied types of narrow themes. For example, the clothes theme in the female set is a broad topic of interest, positive sentiment is a communication attribute and "baby lion" is a very narrow topic. In addition, the male comments tended to be longer, resulting in many common small words, such as conjunctions, appearing in the WAD list. These were grouped into a length theme to account for this.

Figure 6.11 illustrates the one automated and two human processing stages for the female-authored comments. The same stages were carried out for the male-authored comments.

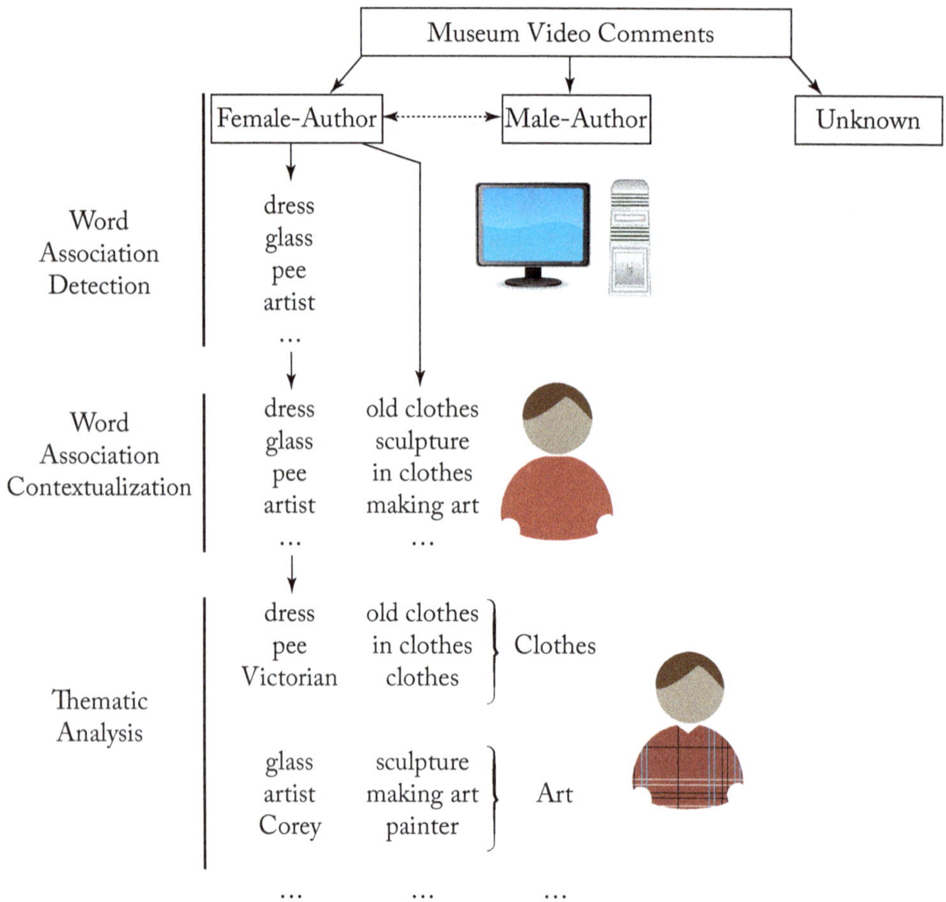

Figure 6.11: The three main stages of word association thematic analysis for the female-authored museum YouTube comments.

Table 6.1: Themes extracted from terms that were female-gendered (3 stars) in 50 YouTube museum channel video comments by exploring their context in comments. The data is the combined comment set from all videos. Singular and plural terms are merged (Thelwall, 2018c)

Theme	Female-Gendered Terms Within the Theme
Clothes	Dress, layer, pocket, dressed, clothes, wear, corset, dresses, jeans, knicker, clothing, wearing, century, bra, outfit, gown, summer, boob, wore, Victorian, pants, fashion, skirt, hair, Dita, Eliza, Hamilton, bathroom, pee, uncomfortable, maid
Positive sentiment	beautiful, love, thank, cute, omg, so, loved, amazing, wonderful, gorgeous, adorable, aww, wow, fascinating, lovely, sharing
Personal	I, my, am, wish, watching
Females	she, her, women, girl
Art	Art, artist, glass, Corey (painting instructor)
Baby lion	Cub
Shop	Woodprix
Vampire bats	bats [How Vampire Bats Suck Blood for 30 Minutes Unnoticed]

Table 6.2: Themes extracted from terms that were male-gendered (3 stars) in 50 YouTube museum channel video comments by exploring their context in comments. The data is the combined comment set from all videos. Singular and plural terms are merged (Thelwall, 2018c)

Theme	Male-Gendered Terms Within the Theme
Military	tank, gun, war, German, Tiger, round, force, plane, bullet, Soviet, aircraft, turret, Sherman, shot, Fletcher (name), Jingle (name)
Argument	nothing, say, shit, far, not, no, theory, if, point, likely, evidence, but, fact, fuck, argument
Universe history	year, simulation, earth, exist, hundred, speed, existence
Science	science, number, thousand, mile, light
Religion	evolution, bible
Space	space, universe
Men	man, guy
Cars	car
Engines	engine
Games	game
Geopolitics	Europe

Computing	system
Things	the, a, an, it, on, in, out [typically used to discuss an object]
Nothing–length-related	of, as, or, which, by, is, there, be, than, we, that, any, at, with, and, from, only, has, into, to, then, one, another, most

6.3 GENDER DIFFERENCES IN ACADEMIC PUBLISHING

Three studies have used WATA to investigate gender difference in research methods and topic choices within academic publishing. They covered the U.S. (Thelwall et al., 2019a), India (Thelwall et al., 2019b), and the UK (Thelwall et al., 2020). These three studies used a range of other methods in different ways but applied WATA in almost the same way. The U.S. case is summarized here and the full texts of preprints of the three papers are all free online.

For the analysis of academic gender differences in research methods and topic choices in academia within U.S., the raw data consisted of the titles, abstracts and keywords of 285,619 journal articles published in 2017 with a U.S. first author, as recorded in the academic database Scopus. The 285,619 texts for the WATA comprised, for each article, the title added to the abstract, added to the keywords (if present) as a single textual unit. These were imported into Mozdeh using the Scopus options accessed through its "Import Data" button. Author genders were detected from their first names, when present, cross-referencing them against U.S. census data saved within Mozdeh. Authors using initials or non-polarized names (e.g., Pat, Alex) were ignored. For the WAD component, Mozdeh formed a list of terms more likely to be in male-authored texts (i.e., title, abstract, keywords) than in female-authored text, and the other way round. This paper made a number of simplifying assumptions, such as that ignoring the genders and national affiliations of authors after the first would not bias the findings. If making such assumptions, it is important to explicitly state and justify them.

For each gender, the top 100 terms were selected for WAA and their meanings and contexts were detected by all the methods described in the WAC chapter. For example, the word "yoga" was found in a higher percentage of female-authored texts than male-authored texts and the WAC identified *yoga* as having the meaning "physical and mental relaxation exercise" (rather than, e.g., spiritual tradition or a particular group), and its context was use within psychotherapy regimes. Another example is "externalizing", which was typically used when discussing psychiatric illnesses, so this was used as its context. Some of the words were academic jargon that had to be looked up in Wikipedia.

An informal thematic analysis was next used to organize the WAA terms into themes, with the results shown in Tables 6.3 and 6.4. Thus, for example, the most female-associated theme was *mothers* (Table 6.3) and the most male-associated theme was *pure mathematics* (Table 6.4).

In this analysis all the words were fitted into different themes, and this tends to be the case for WATA, even if some of the themes overlap. Often in types of thematic analysis, a text can fit multiple themes. This may still have occurred here if words from different themes were in the same journal articles (e.g., *maternal* and *breastfeed* are both in the title of the 2017 article, "Counseling about the maternal health benefits of breastfeeding and mothers' intentions to breastfeed").

The paper reporting the gender WATA for U.S. journal articles did not include the percentage of articles containing each term but instead reported the ratio of the percentage of females using the term to the percentage of males using it (Table 6.4) or the other way round (Table 6.3). This ratio was more informative than reporting two percentages since it encapsulated the difference in a single number. The article deduced that there were substantial fine-grained female-male differences in research topics and method in U.S. academia, at least as expressed through academic journal article publishing.

Table 6.3: The top 100 male-associated academic terms for the overall Scopus 2017 dataset organized by subjectively determined theme. M:F is the proportion of female-authored articles containing the term divided by the proportion of male-authored articles containing the term (Thelwall et al., 2019a)

Theme	M:F*	Statistically Significant Gendered Top 100 Terms (up to 4)**
Pure maths	40/0	Countable, Riemannian, homotopy, axiom…
Engine component	15.74	Coolant, rotor, actuator, rotator,…
Physics	15.59	Relativity, LHC, astrophysical, spacetime,…
Measurement	13.40	Mach
Surgery	12.08	Periprosthetic, arthroscopic, decompression, embolization
Bone surgery	9.72	Arthrodesis, TKA, acetabular, humeral,…
Signal processing	7.45	Interferometer, resonator, khz, mhz, …
Scholarly debate	7.32	Reply, erroneous
Computing	6.53	Arbitrarily, open-source
Medical imaging	6.45	Angiographic
Economics	5.64	Macroeconomic, liquidity, inflation
Engineering	5.04	Vorticity
Religion	4.20	Doctrine

* Divide by 0.809 to get the F/M author ratio

** Ambiguous (e.g., polysemous) terms occurring within multiple possible themes are not shown: PCI, loosening, superposition, rectangular, instabilities, vortex, convective, rotational, mesoscale, drag (e.g., PCI could mean percutaneous coronary intervention or prophylactic cranial irradiation).

Table 6.4: The 100 terms most likely to be used by females in comparison to males for the overall Scopus 2017 dataset (after duplicate article elimination) organized by subjectively determined theme. F:M is the proportion of female-authored articles containing the term divided by the proportion of male-authored articles containing the term (Thelwall et al., 2019a)

Theme	F:M*	Statistically Significant Gendered top 100 terms**
Mothers	15.02	Mothering, motherhood, mother-child, mother, maternal
Babies	13.21	Breastfeed, breastfeeding, birthweight, babies
Children	9.79	Preschool-aged, pre-schooler, childcare, toddler, parenthood, teen, parenting, maltreatment, pubertal
Childbirth	8.65	Pre-pregnancy, childbirth, GDM, postpartum, antenatal, trimester, Cesarean, perinatal, pregnancy, NICU, gestational pregnancies, pregnant, maternity
Women	7.74	Latina's, herself, feminist, feminism, Latina, femininity,
Interpersonal	6.56	Mother-infant, family-centered, parent-child, interprofessional
Talking	6.38	Talked, speech-language, audio-recorded, verbatim, linguistically
Education	5.67	Baccalaureate, service-learning, practicum, preschool, mentoring
Psychiatric illness	5.16	Bulimia, nervosa, eating, trauma-exposed, trauma-informed, telehealth, internalizing, externalizing
Gender inequality	4.25	Sexism, gendered
Sexual violence	3.94	IPV, rape, harassment
Contraception	3.67	Contraception, contraceptive
Female health	3.53	Menopausal, menopause, menstrual, gynecology
Interviews	3.34	Videotaped, facilitator, semistructured, transcribed [see: Talking]
Nursing	3.26	Nursing, nurse
Psychotherapy	3.24	Yoga
Social inequality	3.06	Socioeconomically, intersectionality, sociocultural, underserved
Food health	3.04	Lunch (e.g., national school lunch programmes)
Health management	2.91	Self-management
Language community	2.78	Monolingual, Spanish-speaking
Carers	2.73	Caregiving, caregiver
Survey	2.54	Mailed

* Multiply by 0.809 to get the F/M author ratio.
** Ambiguous (e.g., polysemous) terms occurring within multiple possible themes are not shown: Mulatta, self-perceived, Macaca, culturally, cooking, coaching, work-related (e.g., "Mulatta" occurred in different uses of Macaca mulatta rhesus macaques in experimental and wild contexts).

6.4 INTERNATIONAL DIFFERENCES IN ACADEMIC NURSING PUBLISHING

A different type of study of academic publications used WATA to investigate international differences in nursing topics, relative to the U.S. As in the previous example, the data source was Scopus journal articles. In this case the comparison is based on the national affiliation of the first author (U.S. vs. non-U.S.), rather than their gender. In addition, the results are presented in a list rather than a table, as copied below (Thelwall and Mas-Bleda, in press). The purpose of the paper was to identify research topics that were investigated by U.S. nurses but that had not been published about in other countries. In consequence, all terms might be useful and were listed in full.

- **Age group or patient group:** Several patient types are more mentioned in the U.S., suggesting that research into these groups is more prevalent (pediatric, adolescent, college student, veteran, older adult, geriatric, women).
- **Biochemistry and genetics:** Nursing research in the U.S. seems to be more likely to focus on factors underlying diseases (genetic, genomic, cytokine, cortisol).
- **Disease/illness/health problem/symptoms:** Many diseases are discussed more in the U.S., despite most affecting the countries analyzed similarly (heart failure, HIV, obesity, depressive symptom, symptom, biomarker, hypertension, sickle cell disease, childhood obesity, depression, cognition, sleep, premature infant, fatigue, sexual assault, posttraumatic stress disorder, human papillomavirus, inflammation, HPV, HIV prevention, fall prevention, traumatic brain injury, prematurity, cervical cancer, intimate partner violence, substance abuse, asthma, AIDS, breast cancer, unintended pregnancy, preeclampsia, rape, sleep disturbance).
- **Ethnicity or ethnic sensitivity:** It is not surprising that terms related to U.S. demographics are less used in other English-speaking nations (African American, Hispanic, Latino, African American women, Asian American, Mexican American, Korean American, black). Two terms are not demographic-specific but relate to strategies in the U.S. for effective nursing of multicultural populations (acculturation, cultural competency).

- **Location for nursing or type of nursing:** Except for the last example, these are due to U.S.-specific terminology (high school, NICU [neonatal intensive care unit], primary care).

- **Nurse education/training:** Nursing education seems to have a focus in the U.S. (nursing education, teaching strategies, graduate nursing education, faculty [a term less used outside the U.S.] development) and some terms point to the organization of education (QSEN [Quality and Safety Education for Nurses]) or U.S.-specific educational strategies (standardized patient, service-learning, simulation).

- Nurse skills, tasks, competencies and strategies: General nursing skills seem to be more commonly referenced in the U.S. (evidence-based practice, measurement, patient education, holistic nursing, safe patient handling).

- **Nursing administration or management:** There are many relatively unique administration-related terms for the U.S., presumably because countries organize health systems differently (electronic health record, quality improvement, emergency preparedness, shared governance, care coordination, nurse staffing, electronic medical record, Omaha system [taxonomy designed to describe client care], process improvement).

- **Nursing qualification or role:** There are international differences in terminology for roles and qualifications (Advanced Practice Nurse, Nurse Practitioner, APN [Advanced Practice Nurse], Advanced Practice Registered Nurse, Doctor Of Nursing Practice, school nurse, nursing faculty, clinical nurse leader, certification, school nursing, NCLEX-RN [National Council Licensure Examination for Registered Nurses], faculty, nurse faculty).

- **Nursing theory:** Two theories and theory in general are more mentioned in the U.S. (human becoming, Parse (person), nursing theory, Roy Adaptation Model).

- **Research methods:** Three research methods are more used in the U.S. (community-based participatory research, concept analysis, instrument development).

- **Social perspectives about health:** Wider social issues surrounding the health of individuals seem to be discussed more in the U.S. (health disparities, women's health, health literacy, global health, disparities, environmental health, diversity, transcultural health, health policy, Africa).

- **Technology in nursing:** Computing technology seems to be more mentioned in the U.S. (informatics, nursing informatics, technology, health information technology), including one application (teledermatology).

- **Treatment, care, diagnostic tools:** Several of these are more discussed in the U.S. (physical activity, exercise, contraception, DNP [DiNitroPhenol diet drug], symptom management, prenatal care, hospice, cesarean birth, radiation therapy, vaccine, mammography, caregiver, self-care, medication adherence).

- **Generic:** Two terms had multiple uses (nursing science, elementary).

6.5 SUMMARY

This chapter summarized the data and WATA results of some published journal articles. The data sources include Twitter, YouTube, and academic publications. The reporting methods include graphs, tables, and bullet point lists. In some cases, WATA was the primary result reported in the paper but in other articles included additional descriptive information. The applications therefore span multiple fields and data sources and report the findings in different ways, but exploit the same core method.

CHAPTER 7

Comparison Between WATA and Other Methods

This chapter compares word association thematic analysis with other social research methods used to analyze texts. This can help a decision about which method is the most appropriate to use as well as highlighting the relative strengths and weaknesses of all methods. Each technique has one or more programs that can be used to support it. For example, Nvivo might be used for content analysis or thematic analysis. In addition, many social media research projects combine a range of methods to support an argument or investigate a context (e.g., Rogers, 2020), and there are qualitative methods designed to cope with large volumes of texts (e.g., Davidson et al., 2019).

7.1 CONTENT ANALYSIS

Content analysis is a method to organize things into well-defined categories through subjective judgements (Neuendorf, 2016). For this, one or more coders reads the set of texts, then decides on an appropriate set of categories for them. They name and define the categories carefully and then categorize all the texts with these categories. The result of this process is information about the percentage of texts that match each category. For example, a content analysis applied to a set of U.S. newspaper stories about the science of Covid-19 might find that 25% discuss the psychology of lockdown, 50% discuss progress with vaccines, and 25% discuss possible treatments and cures. An advantage of content analysis compared to versions of thematic analysis is that the coders can categorize the texts into the categories independently, allowing tests of inter-coder consistency to be reported, justifying the validity of the categories. A second advantage of content analysis is that it can report direct prevalence percentages for the texts (e.g., 50% discuss progress).

An important difference between content analysis and WATA is that WATA centers on differences between subsets whereas content analysis describes the entire set. Thus, content analysis might be less effective at characterizing the main differences in a set of texts (e.g., male vs. female; high scoring vs. low scoring; positive sentiment vs. the rest). In contrast, WATA can't describe a set of texts overall unless there is another set to contrast it against. For example, one WATA study focused on tweets about attention deficit hyperactivity disorder (ADHD) by contrasting them with other disease and disorder tweets (Thelwall et al., 2021).

A second difference between content analysis and WATA is that WATA focuses on words, their meanings, and contexts. WATA results are therefore about the existence of meanings and contexts within a set of texts rather than the typical meaning of individual texts. Related to this, a third difference is that WATA does not produce direct prevalence information: it reports that themes are more discussed in one subset than another and can report the percentage of texts in each set that contain an individual word, but this falls short of estimating the prevalence of the themes identified.

7.2 THEMATIC ANALYSIS

Thematic analysis is a method to detect themes within collections of things (Braun and Clarke, 2013, 2006). It works by one or more coders reading a set of texts, then tagging the texts with multiple possible themes, and then repeatedly revisiting the texts and themes, organizing them and comparing them until a coherent set of themes emerges that characterizes some important properties of the collection. In contrast to content analysis, and like WATA, its aim is not to identify prevalence information for the themes but to identify the core themes within a collection.

Like content analysis, thematic analysis characterizes a collection of documents rather than looking for differences between subsets. Also like content analysis, it focuses to a large extent on texts rather than words. These are two important differences with WATA.

One study has compared WATA to thematic analysis on a set of tweets from people claiming to have Attention Deficit Hyperactivity Disorder (ADHD), using different investigators to apply each method independently (Thelwall et al., 2021). The WATA used a set of tweets about people discussing 99 other disorders for its comparison set. The results suggested that standard (reflexive) thematic analysis is better at identifying general themes, whereas WATA may identify more themes, including fine-grained themes that would be very hard to detect with standard thematic analysis because they are rare. Thus, a key advantage of WATA is its ability to identify rare themes through its word frequency comparison approach.

7.3 WORD CLOUDS

A word cloud is not a social research method but is sometimes visualize the contents of one or more documents. A word cloud is a picture in which the most common words in a document or set are illustrated, with the size of a word being proportional to its frequency (Hearst et al., 2019). Common words, such as "the" and "it" are usually removed. This is an artistic way to get insights into the content of a document but is essentially the same as a long table or bar chart listing the frequency of each word in a document. It does not reveal major categories or themes and does not identify differences between document sets.

7.4 TOP HASHTAGS

Investigating the most used hashtags in a collection of tweets can give insights into organized or focused tweeting, especially if they are widely used and give clear context. For example, one study found that #BlackLivesMatter and #TCOT indicated opposing sides of a debate about racism (Ray et al., 2017). In such contests, top hashtags could be discussed alongside WATA or other analyses.

7.5 DOCUMENT CLUSTERING

Document clustering is a broad computer science or statistical method to identify document-level patterns within sets of documents (Abualigah, Khader, and Hanandeh, 2018). Document clustering organizes a set of documents into clusters so that sets of documents within a cluster tend to have similar contents to each other, but different contents to documents in other clusters. This is achieved with the help of a mathematical formula that estimates the topic similarity of pairs of documents through the extent that they use the same words. Each cluster might then be labeled by a person or an algorithm. Thus, for example, a document clustering applied to a set of ADHD tweets might produce separate clusters about school experiences, medication and parental reactions.

Like content analysis, document clustering works at the level of whole documents. Its advantage is that it is fully automatic and therefore quick. A disadvantage is that its automatic nature can cause it to create clusters that make little sense and it can miss useful clusters. A second disadvantage is that there is no statistical support for the clusters—small changes in a set of documents can produce completely different clusters.

7.6 DOCUMENT SET MAPPING

Document set mapping is another broad method to identify document-level patterns within sets of documents. Document mapping is an automatic technique, like document clustering, but the output is a two-dimensional map in which each document is a point on the map and documents are placed close together when their contents are similar (e.g., science document mapping: Chen, 2017). Document mapping is preferable to document clustering when the set contains documents with more of a continuum of topics rather than discrete sets of topics. Document set mapping works well for visualizing academic research areas through their journal articles, for example, because academic topics tend to overlap through interdisciplinary research. Other than this, document set mapping has similar strengths and limitations to document clustering.

7.7 TOPIC MODELING

Topic Modeling is an automatic method for discovering topics (similar to themes in WATA) within sets of documents (Silge and Robinson, 2017). It starts by assuming that (a) the topics exist and (b) each topic is characterized by probabilities to include a set of words. For example, a Cats topic would have high probabilities for including cat-related words, such as *cat*, *feline*, and *meow*. The algorithm both detects the topics and estimates the extent to which each topic is present in each document. An advantage of topic modeling over document set clustering or mapping is that it does not assume that each document contains only one topic because the topic Modeling algorithm allows documents to contain multiple topics. A second advantage is that it can report connections between topics and documents. A speed advantage of topic modeling over WATA is that the topics are identified automatically, although they are usually be labeled manually (some automatic methods exist to suggest labels). As for document set clustering, some topics can make no sense and there is no statistical support for the results: small changes in the data can produce large changes in the topics.

Topic modeling is similar to WATA in that it identifies a set of topics/themes based on word frequencies, although the idea is to characterize the main topics within a single set of documents rather than to compare two sets of documents. Topic modeling results are not based on statistical tests, however, and should be interpreted as a perspective on the data, rather than statistical evidence of the existence of the topics found.

7.8 TEXT/SEMANTIC NETWORKS

Some methods convert sets of documents into networks, where the nodes are important words and these words/nodes are connected by lines when they tend to occur in the same document. The network can also be automatically clustered to identify themes through collections of related words (Segev, 2020). For this method to work well, the words in the network need to be manually selected, not only to ignore common terms (e.g., *it*, *the*) but also to focus on terms that are most relevant to the issue analyzed.

Semantic networks offer a similar approach (Drieger, 2013; Tang et al., 2018), also illustrating a set of documents with a network of key words, with lines in the network connecting words that tend to occur in the same texts. This strategy has been used to compare reactions to a Korean mayoral TV debate through Facebook, Twitter, and blogs (Heo et al., 2016) and to analyze a topic on Twitter in Korea (Kim, Lee, and Park, 2016).

An important advantage of text networks is that the structure of the themes can be seen through the connections between component words, and these same connections can be used to identify relationships between themes. As with the other automatic methods discussed here, the disadvantages are a lack of a statistical test for any aspect of the model, a lack of human control over the final themes, and the possibility that small changes in the document set could make large changes in the results.

7.9 NATURAL LANGUAGE PROCESSING AND PRE-PROCESSING POSSIBILITIES

Text is sometimes pre-processed to perform tasks like correcting typos, expanding acronyms, and removing common words (called stopwords). Mozdeh does not do this because it is designed primarily for informal social web texts, where typos may be deliberate, acronyms may be new inventions and common words may be important to text processing (e.g., *I* and *you* are often identified by Mozdeh as gendered terms). Additional pro-processing to remove typos (before importing text into Mozdeh) may be considered if a set of texts has relatively many non-deliberate typos for some reason. An important limitation is that it ignores all types of emoji altogether, except that it processes text-based emoticons within its sentiment detection. Emojis mostly convey positive sentiment (Novak et al., 2015).

The WAD stage of WATA in Mozdeh has one pre-processing step, however it converts plural words to singular by removing any final "*s*." It otherwise does not merge related words or fit words into common phrases for analysis. Both are possible with natural language processing software and could, in theory, improve the results. Some of these text pre-processing techniques may be used in variants of the alternative methods discussed in this chapter, and two are briefly reviewed here.

- **Lemmatization:** This converts different versions of a word (its inflected forms) into a single, standard format. For example, *run*, *runs*, running, and *ran* would all transform into the base lemma *run*. This pre-processing step can make text-processing algorithms more powerful by allowing them to treat words with different versions as identical. A disadvantage is that the different versions of a word might be important for some analyses (e.g., a focus on the present rather than the past).

- **Noun phrase parsing:** This identifies noun phrases in a text and converts them into single objects for processing. For example, the sentence "I went to the Bank of England" contains the noun phrase "the Bank of England" which can be understood as a single entity with a clear meaning. Noun phrase parsing would convert this sentence to "I went to the-Bank-of-England", with four objects rather than seven words. A disadvantage is that the constituent words might be more important. For example, in discussions about lots of different banks, the word "Bank" might be more useful to analyze than the phrase "the Bank of England".

For WATA, the above variants made little difference to the end results in the only systematic comparison so far (Thelwall and Mas-Bleda, in press). They also make the algorithm much slower, so are not used by Mozdeh.

It is likely that lemmatization or noun phrase parsing (or part of speech tagging: annotating words with their grammatical function) will improve the word association results for some topics, despite the above finding. In particular, noun phrase parsing may be beneficial when noun phrases, such as the names of people or places, are central to the topic investigated and the constituent words are not distinctive. To illustrate this, an analysis of musicians on Twitter might lose information about prominent performers like Lady Gaga whose names (e.g., "Lady Gaga") are unique to them, whereas their constituent words (*Lady* and *Gaga*) aren't. This is mitigated on Twitter by usernames being unique (e.g., @ladygaga) but performers are not always tweeted about with their usernames.

Natural language processing techniques like lemmatization, noun phrase parsing, and part of speech tagging all have the potential to improve WAD by connecting terms more closely to their meanings. Their main disadvantages are that they are slow for large sections of text, they are error-prone (particularly for informal social web language), and they add a layer of abstraction that can obscure the meaning of texts. For these reasons, they are recommended only when they have clear advantages for a particular topic.

Although Mozdeh does not support lemmatization or noun phrase parsing, there are many free toolkits for this (Manning et al., 2014; Qi et al., 2020). Text processed with these methods (or with other pre-processing) can then be imported for processing by Mozdeh, as long as the tagging method creates alphanumeric words (e.g., converting "Lady Gaga" to Lady-Gaga or Lady_Gaga but not to <np>Lady Gaga</np> because of the space in the phrase).

7.10 CORPUS-ASSISTED CRITICAL DISCOURSE ANALYSIS

Other research approaches exist for analyzing sets of text with objectives that are similar to WATA. Corpus-Assisted Critical Discourse Analysis (CACDA) combines the quantitative methods of corpus linguistics with the critical discourse analysis goal of studying the use of discourse (spoken or written text) to investigate power relations in society (Baker et al., 2008). This approach uses a range of methods in an iterative process, attempting to identify themes and structure in the texts. It is more exploratory that WATA, employing a wider variety of methods and is not based on statistical tests. The advantage of CACDA is its flexibility, which may be necessary to identify power relations, but this makes its findings less robust and more exploratory. It also lacks the thematic analysis stage of WATA. In practice, however, a CACDA can focus on similar word frequency comparisons to WATA (e.g., Wang, 2018), so the methods overlap.

7.11 SUMMARY

This chapter has briefly discussed some of the many text analysis methods for social research, each with strengths and weaknesses. This section summarizes the strengths and weaknesses of WATA compared to these.

The most important difference between WATA and the methods discussed above is that WATA analyzes differences between subsets within a text collection rather than the whole collection. It is therefore more suitable for addressing questions of difference. It can also investigate collections of texts by splitting them into subsets or analysis, such as based on texts that are high/low scoring, positive or negative, posted early or late, male or female authored). If a reference set of similar texts is available, then comparing the set with the reference collection allows a descriptive analysis, however. WATA is unsuitable for producing an overall description of a set of texts when no reference set of texts is available.

An important advantage of WATA over automated methods is that it starts with a set of statistically significant terms. Even though it includes subjective stages of meaning and context detection, then thematic analysis, it is grounded in statistically significant differences. In contrast, automated methods can find patterns even in random texts, so they can mislead the researcher into thinking that patterns exist when there are none.

The concept of statistical significance for patterns is less relevant to content analysis and thematic analysis but an advantage of WATA over both of these is that the starting point of a set of terms that occur more in one set than another points the researcher conducting the TA part of WATA to points of difference. As a result, the WATA analyst asks the question "why is this word more common in a subset?" rather than "what is a key aspect of this text?" This can be helpful because the "why" question guides the analyst by being more specific than the "what" question. This drove a WATA analyzing discussions of bullying in YouTube influencers' comments to identify generalization-based support as a common but non-obvious theme (Thelwall and Cash, to appear).

WATA has important disadvantages compared to other methods. At a practical level, it requires learning software and is only currently supported by the Windows program Mozdeh. It can overlook themes that are not reflected in word use differences and does not give theme prevalence information (unlike content analysis).

CHAPTER 8

Ethics

Any project analyzing human-generated texts needs to consider its ethical implications. The relevant considerations depend on the source and the nature of the texts, including any reasonable expectations to privacy for the text authors. There is no consensus on ethical uses of social media data (Samuel, Derrick, and van Leeuwen, 2019) so it is important to consider a variety of perspectives. This chapter makes the case for analyzing public social web texts not requiring explicit consent from post authors, although not all researchers agree (Golder et al., 2017).

8.1 IS PERMISSION REQUIRED TO ANALYZE PUBLIC TEXTS?

Most social science research projects involving interviews, surveys, or questionnaires would require explicit informed consent from all participants, but this does not necessarily apply to studies of human-created public texts.

Although each case should be considered on its own merits, in general terms, if someone posts to the public web (e.g., twitter.com, YouTube.com, or anywhere else that does not require logon) then their post may be considered to be in the public domain and permission is not required to analyze it (Eysenbach and Till, 2001; Wilkinson and Thelwall, 2011). The situation is different for websites that require a logon, such as private Facebook pages, because participants might reasonably expect that their contributions are not used, however indirectly, by anyone that is not a member of the appropriate community or that they have not given access permission to. Thus, for fully public texts, such as tweets and YouTube comments, posts can be treated to a large extent as public domain in the same way as books are public domain: a researcher would not need to ask permission of an author to investigate their book. The rationale for this is that putting something fully in the public domain entails implicit consent for people to use it in ways that the creator might not know about or might not like.

The same general exception for public social web posts applies to all other public datasets fed into Mozdeh. The academic text analyses described above, for example, used the titles, abstracts, and keywords of thousands of academic journal articles without asking permission from their authors. This is reasonable because journal articles are placed by publishers into the public domain. Even if they are closed access, their titles, abstracts, and keywords are almost always public, such as on journal websites.

If text fed into Mozdeh is from a non-public source, then author consent may be required to analyze it. Careful consideration should then be given to an appropriate form for this consent (Markham and Buchanan, 2012) and approval sought from appropriate ethical review committees.

8.2 CAN POSTERS BE NAMED OR QUOTED?

In general, author identities should not be revealed for public texts, unless they are public figures, or the text is a formal publication. This is an important point because naming a person, even for something apparently innocuous, might cause them harm. In all cases, a person with a hidden mental health disorder might become distressed if they are mentioned, irrespective of what they posted about. It is therefore a sensible precaution not to name people or their usernames. This book includes exact quotes only from journal articles because these are formal publications. Identifying authors of formal publications, such as books, is accepted practice in academia.

Not naming a private person extends to not quoting their post (Eysenbach and Till, 2001; Wilkinson and Thelwall, 2011). This is because a web author could be discovered by searching for their post in Google, the hosting social web service, or a commercial text mining service. For this reason, all quotes should be modified substantially to the extent that even the owner would not recognize the quote if it was pointed out to them. This can be achieved by merging two or more quotes, changing most of the words and the word orders. Thus, the most important ethical consideration for a typical social web project is to ensure that it is impossible to identify the post authors from any publication reporting the analysis.

It seems reasonable to ignore the above rules for people that are public figures, such as elected politicians and major celebrities. Someone in this role effectively gives up their right to privacy for their public posts. A case could also be made for mentioning the identity of a non-public figure if it is already well known and published in the context of the posts analyzed. For example, if a member of the public triggered extensive press coverage through their actions and responded on Twitter, it seems reasonable to include their name and quotes since their identity is fully in the public domain.

8.3 SUMMARY

This chapter has argued that explicit author approval is not needed to analyze public texts, such as tweets, YouTube comment, or academic journal articles, although it would be needed to analyze private texts. Nevertheless, the identities of the text authors should not be revealed, and exact quotes should be strictly avoided, except in the special cases mentioned above. Researchers should always consult their local ethical guidelines and committees to ensure compliance and guard against unexpected sources of problems, however.

CHAPTER 9

Project Planning

Careful planning for a WATA (or WAA) can minimize the risks of a project. The two main risks are an inability to collect enough high-quality data or collecting it too late, and insufficient statistically significant WAD terms.

Goals: Any research project should start by delineating its goals. What is the purpose of the analysis? What type of results might emerge from it? Are there any expectations from the results? For WATA it helps if there is some flexibility in the goals so that the methods can be adjusted to give the greatest chance of interesting findings. User demographics should also be clarified at the goals stage, by language and (usually) nationality or country location. Ethical issues should be considered at this stage.

Method selection: The next stage is choosing a method to address these goals. WATA is suitable if the goals can be addressed by collecting and analyzing a large set of texts to identify and characterize differences between subsets (e.g., male vs. female, high vs. low scoring, positive vs. negative sentiment, early vs. late, one subtopic vs. another). To illustrate this, if the goal is to identify gender differences in public reactions to Covid-19 events in social media, then WATA applied to Covid-19 would be appropriate. It is also suitable to compare one set of texts against a reference set. A project may employ multiple methods to give different perspectives.

Testing for sufficient data: Before starting full-scale data collection, it is important to assess whether there will be enough relevant posts (at least 10,000 for a tightly focused set of texts, otherwise 100,000+). This can be checked by querying on twitter.com for relevant tweets to estimate how many there are. It is possible to estimate the number of tweets per day by counting how many of the most recent matching tweets were in the past hour, then multiplying by 24. This figure can then be used to estimate the number of tweets that could be collected over the time available for data collection (e.g., a week, three months). This gives an insight into whether enough texts could be collected in time. If this looks unlikely, then the alternatives include choosing another research goal, widening the research goal to allow more texts to be collected or using a different data source or analysis method. If data collection is planned for a future event (e.g., International Women's Day) then this step will not be possible, unless data is available from the same event in a previous year. If older tweets are needed for the analysis then permission should be sought from Twitter's Academic Research offering (https://developer.twitter.com/en/solutions/academic-research) as soon as possible. An early successful application will allow the project to assess the amount of tweets available from this extended source and plan accordingly.

Query generation: The pilot testing stage involves creating the queries (or usernames) for the main data collection stage. As discussed above, this may be straightforward (e.g., projects based around individuals or hashtags) or require a lot of work (e.g., projects based around concepts or broad topics). For the main data collection, the data must be high quality in the sense of containing little spam or other irrelevant content. If queries are used to collect the texts (e.g., from Twitter) then a week may be needed to generate a collection of high precision queries with a low percentage of irrelevant matches. For a future event the queries could not be tested in advance for precision, unless data from previous years is available. Without this testing research may be needed to identify likely terms and hashtags for the main data collection. If necessary, tweets matching low precision queries could be filtered out by Mozdeh after the main data collection stage.

Data collection: Once the queries are ready, Mozdeh can collect texts continuously for as long as necessary but it should be checked daily to guard against Windows crashes or automatic restarts. If a project is based around an event known about in advance (e.g., International Women's Day) then the data collection should be started at least 24 hours before the day starts to capture initial posts in other parts of the world and to ensure that no posts are missed even if the focus is on one country. For the same reason, the collection should continue until 24 hours after the end of the day. Consideration should be given to longer-term data collection to capture planning events and longer-term reactions. Contemporary data collection may not be necessary if access is granted to older tweets for academic research by Twitter.

Waiting: Assuming that the data collection is a long-term exercise, other research tasks can be undertaken while waiting for it to finish, such as organizing the analysis team (if not a solo effort), updating the literature review, and becoming familiar with the Mozdeh processing options. In addition, a formal or informal project plan can be made based on the planned data collection duration.

WAD: Once the data collection is complete, Mozdeh can be used to generate lists of statistically significant terms for each subset analyzed in the data (i.e., WAD). Depending on the number of statistically significant terms, a decision must be made about whether to analyze them all, or as many as necessary, stopping when theme saturation has been achieved.

WAC and TA: The next stage is WAC: identifying the meanings and contexts of the statistically significant terms. This involves using Mozdeh to generate random samples of texts containing the terms and follow-up word association list generation. TA is next, grouping the terms into coherent themes. Returning to the previous stage to contextualize additional words is part of this.

Writing up: The final stage is writing up the results, avoiding naming people or giving exact quotes, except for public figures or other exceptional cases. The chapter with examples includes different ways of presenting the results, including a series of figures (one per theme), a table, or a bullet point list.

CHAPTER 10

Summary

This book describes two related methods to analyze collections of texts, Word Association Analysis and Word Association Thematic Analysis. They are most useful for a project when the goal is to find differences between subsets. It is important to ensure high-quality data for WATA and therefore the initial text collection stage should be conducted carefully to ensure that the overwhelming majority of the texts collected are relevant to the project as far as possible, whether from the social web or elsewhere. WATA and WAA can be applied to research problems that can be addressed by analyzing sets of texts and either looking for differences within the texts (e.g., male-authored vs. female-authored) or characterizing the texts relative to a reference set (e.g., ADHD tweets compared to other health-related tweets). The methods have strengths and weaknesses compared to other text analysis methods used in the social sciences and humanities. The main strengths are the potential to point to aspects of difference that human checking could miss, and the statistical basis for the WAD stage of the method.

WAA starts by detecting lists of words that are statistically significantly percentage of texts in one subset than another (the WAD stage with Mozdeh), then detects the meaning and context of those words within the collection (the WAC stage):

$$\text{WAA} = \text{WAD} + \text{WAC}$$

WATA is a large sample extension of WAA. A thematic analysis is necessary if there are more than 15–25 words from WAA because this is too many to discuss individually. WATA starts with WAA and then TA organizes the words detected into narrow themes, characterizing a range of differences within the collection. Themes may encompass words with different associations (e.g., both male and female). If there are many narrow themes, then these may be organized into broad themes. WATA is the sum of its three main stages, after data collection:

$$\text{WATA} = \text{WAD} + \text{WAC} + \text{TA}$$

The WAA part of WATA is supported by the Windows software Mozdeh, which (at the time of writing) collects tweets and YouTube comments, as well as importing texts from other sources. Once fed into Mozdeh, the texts can be split into subsets in multiple different ways for WATA. Mozdeh supports the WAC stage by producing lists of random texts containing the word to read, and by producing follow-up word association lists.

This book has described WAA and WATA so that they can be used to tackle new research problems. I hope that you find them useful for your project and they help you find information that would have been invisible to other methods.

References

Abualigah, L. M., Khader, A. T., and Hanandeh, E. S. (2018). A combination of objective functions and hybrid krill herd algorithm for text document clustering analysis. *Engineering Applications of Artificial Intelligence*, 73, 111–125. DOI: 10.1016/j.engappai.2018.05.003. 93

Ahmed, W., Bath, P. A., Sbaffi, L., and Demartini, G. (2018). Measuring the effect of public health campaigns on Twitter: the case of World Autism Awareness Day. In *International Conference on Information* (pp. 10–16). Berlin, Germany: Springer, Cham. DOI: 10.1007/978-3-319-78105-1_2. 14

atilika (2014). *Kuromoji*. https://www.atilika.org/. 11

Baker, P., Gabrielatos, C., Khosravinik, M., Krzyżanowski, M., McEnery, T., and Wodak, R. (2008). A useful methodological synergy? Combining critical discourse analysis and corpus linguistics to examine discourses of refugees and asylum seekers in the UK press. *Discourse and Society*, 19(3), 273–306.DOI: 10.1177/0957926508088962. 96

Bednarek, M. (2019). "Don't say crap. Don't use swear words." Negotiating the use of swear/taboo words in the narrative mass media. *Discourse, Context and Media*, 29, 100293.DOI: 10.1016/j.dcm.2019.02.002. 43

Benjamini, Y. and Hochberg, Y. (1995). Controlling the false discovery rate: a practical and powerful approach to multiple testing. *Journal of the Royal Statistical Society: Series B (Methodological)*, 57(1), 289–300.DOI: 10.1111/j.2517-6161.1995.tb02031.x. 37

Braun, V. and Clarke, V. (2006). Using thematic analysis in psychology. *Qualitative Research in Psychology*, 3(2), 77–101.DOI: 10.1191/1478088706qp063oa. 61, 92

Braun, V. and Clarke, V. (2013). *Successful Qualitative Research: A Practical Guide for Beginners*. London, UK: Sage. 61, 92

Braun, V. and Clarke, V. (2019). To saturate or not to saturate? Questioning data saturation as a useful concept for thematic analysis and sample-size rationales. *Qualitative Research in Sport, Exercise and Health*, 1–16. DOI: 10.1080/2159676X.2019.1704846. 9, 63

Cambridge Dictionary (2020). Structural. https://dictionary.cambridge.org/dictionary/english/structural. 3

Chen, C. (2017). Science mapping: a systematic review of the literature. *Journal of Data and Information Science*, 2(2), 1–40. DOI: 10.1515/jdis-2017-0006. 93

Chernyaev, A., Spryiskov, A., Ivashko, A., and Bidulya, Y. (2020). A rumor detection in Russian tweets. In *International Conference on Speech and Computer* (pp. 108–118). Berlin, Germany: Springer, Cham. DOI: 10.1007/978-3-030-60276-5_11. 16

Creswell, J. W., Plano Clark, V. L., Gutmann, M., and Hanson, W. (2003). Advanced mixed methods research designs. In A. Tashakkori and C. Teddlie (Eds.), *Handbook of Mixed Methods in Social and Behavioral Research* (pp. 209–240). Thousand Oaks, CA: Sage. 8

Davidson, E., Edwards, R., Jamieson, L., and Weller, S. (2019). Big data, qualitative style: a breadth-and-depth method for working with large amounts of secondary qualitative data. *Quality and Quantity*, 53(1), 363–376. DOI: 10.1007/s11135-018-0757-y. 91

Drieger, P. (2013). Semantic network analysis as a method for visual text analytics. *Procedia-Social and Behavioral Sciences*, 79(2013), 4–17. DOI: 10.1016/j.sbspro.2013.05.053. 94

Ette, M. and Joe, S. (2018). "Rival visions of reality": An analysis of the framing of Boko Haram in Nigerian newspapers and Twitter. *Media, War and Conflict,* 11(4), 392–406. DOI: 10.1177/1750635218776560. 14

Eysenbach, G. and Till, J. E. (2001). Ethical issues in qualitative research on internet communities. *BMJ*, 323(7321), 1103–1105. DOI: 10.1136/bmj.323.7321.1103. 99, 100Golder, S., Ahmed, S., Norman, G., and Booth, A. (2017). Attitudes toward the ethics of research using social media: a systematic review. *Journal of Medical Internet Research*, 19(6), e195. DOI: 10.2196/jmir.7082. 99

Guest, G., Namey, E., and Chen, M. (2020). A simple method to assess and report thematic saturation in qualitative research. *PLoS One*, 15(5), e0232076. DOI: 10.1371/journal.pone.0232076. 63

Hearst, M., Pedersen, E., Patil, L. P., Lee, E., Laskowski, P., and Franconeri, S. (2019). An evaluation of semantically grouped word cloud designs. *IEEE Transactions on Visualization and Computer Graphics*, 26(9), 2748–2761. DOI: 10.1109/TVCG.2019.2904683. 92

Heo, Y. C., Park, J. Y., Kim, J. Y., and Park, H. W. (2016). The emerging viewertariat in South Korea: The Seoul mayoral TV debate on Twitter, Facebook, and blogs. *Telematics and Informatics*, 33(2), 570–583. DOI: h10.1016/j.tele.2015.08.003. 94

Holmberg, K. and Hellsten, I. (2015). Gender differences in the climate change communication on Twitter. *Internet Research*, 25(5), 811–828. DOI: 10.1108/IntR-07-2014-0179. 14

Johnson, R. B., Onwuegbuzie, A. J., and Turner, L. A. (2007). Toward a definition of mixed methods research. *Journal of Mixed Methods Research*, 1(2), 112–133. DOI: 10.1177/1558689806298224. 8

Kim, B. (2020). Effects of social grooming on incivility in COVID-19. *Cyberpsychology, Behavior, and Social Networking*. 23(8), 519–525. DOI: 10.1089/cyber.2020.0201. 16

Kim, J., Lee, Y. O., and Park, H. W. (2016). Delineating the complex use of a political podcast in South Korea by hybrid web indicators: The case of the Nakkomsu Twitter network. *Technological Forecasting and Social Change*, 110, 42–50. DOI: 10.1016/j.techfore.2015.11.012. 94

Makita, M., Mas-Bleda, A., Morris, S., and Thelwall, M. (2020). Mental health discourses on Twitter during Mental Health Awareness Week. *Issues in Mental Health Nursing*. DOI: 10.1080/01612840.2020.1814914. 13

Manning, C. D., Surdeanu, M., Bauer, J., Finkel, J. R., Bethard, S., and McClosky, D. (2014). The Stanford CoreNLP natural language processing toolkit. In *Proceedings of 52nd Annual Meeting of The Association For Computational Linguistics: System Demonstrations* (pp. 55–60). DOI: 10.3115/v1/P14-5010. 96

Markham, A. and Buchanan, E. (2012). Ethical decision-making and internet research: Version 2.0. https://aoir.org/reports/ethics2.pdf. 100

Neuendorf, K. A. (2016). *The Content Analysis Guidebook*. Oxford, UK: Sage. DOI: 10.4135/9781071802878. 9, 69, 91

Novak, P. K., Smailović, J., Sluban, B., and Mozetič, I. (2015). Sentiment of emojis. *PloS One*, 10(12), e0144296. DOI: 10.1371/journal.pone.0144296. 95

O'Brien, B. C., Harris, I. B., Beckman, T. J., Reed, D. A., and Cook, D. A. (2014). Standards for reporting qualitative research: a synthesis of recommendations. *Academic Medicine*, 89(9), 1245–1251. DOI: 10.1097/ACM.0000000000000388. 69

Ozduzen, O. and Korkut, U. (2020). Enmeshing the mundane and the political: Twitter, LGBTI+ outing and macro-political polarisation in Turkey. *Contemporary Politics*. DOI: 10.1080/13569775.2020.1759883. 14

Ozduzen, O. and McGarry, A. (2020). Digital traces of "Twitter Revolutions": Resistance, polarization, and surveillance via contested images and texts of occupy Gezi. *International Journal of Communication*, 14, 21. https://ijoc.org/index.php/ijoc/article/view/12400/3080. 16

Potts, G. and Radford, D. R. (2019). #Teeth&Tweets: the reach and reaction of an online social media oral health promotion campaign. *British Dental Journal*, 227(3), 217–222. DOI: 10.1038/s41415-019-0593-z. 13

Qi, P., Zhang, Y., Zhang, Y., Bolton, J., and Manning, C. D. (2020). Stanza: A python natural language processing toolkit for many human languages. *arXiv preprint* arXiv:2003.07082. DOI: 10.18653/v1/2020.acl-demos.14. 96

Ray, R., Brown, M., Fraistat, N., and Summers, E. (2017). Ferguson and the death of Michael Brown on Twitter: #BlackLivesMatter, #TCOT, and the evolution of collective identities. *Ethnic and Racial Studies*, 40(11), 1797–1813. DOI: 10.1080/01419870.2017.1335422. 93

Rogers, R. (2020). Deplatforming: Following extreme Internet celebrities to Telegram and alternative social media. *European Journal of Communication*. DOI: 10.1177/0267323120922066. 91

Ryan, G. W. and Bernard, H. R. (2003). Techniques to identify themes. *Field Methods*, 15(1), 85–109. DOI: 10.1177/1525822X02239569. 61

Samuel, G., Derrick, G., and van Leeuwen, T. N. (2019). Ethical challenges around the use of social media data: Views of researchers and research ethics committee members. https://osf.io/msyb6/download. DOI: 10.31235/osf.io/msyb6. 99

Scherr, S., Arendt, F., Frissen, T., and Oramas M, J. (2020). Detecting intentional self-harm on Instagram: development, testing, and validation of an automatic image-recognition algorithm to discover cutting-related posts. *Social Science Computer Review*, 38(6), 673–685. DOI: 10.1177/0894439319836389. 20

Schoonenboom, J. and Johnson, R. B. (2017). How to construct a mixed methods research design. *KZfSS Kölner Zeitschrift für Soziologie und Sozialpsychologie*, 69(2), 107–131. DOI: 10.1007/s11577-017-0454-1. 8

Segev, E. (2020). Textual network analysis: Detecting prevailing themes and biases in international news and social media. *Sociology Compass*, 14(4), e12779. DOI: 10.1111/soc4.12779. 94

Silge, J. and Robinson, D. (2017). *Text Mining with R: A Tidy Approach*. O'Reilly Media, Inc. 93

Tang, L., Bie, B., and Zhi, D. (2018). Tweeting about measles during stages of an outbreak: A semantic network approach to the framing of an emerging infectious disease. *American Journal of Infection Control*, 46(12), 1375–1380. DOI: 10.1016/j.ajic.2018.05.019. 94

Thelwall, M., Abdoli, M., Lebiedziewicz, A. and Bailey, C. (2020). Gender disparities in UK research publishing: Differences between fields, methods and topics. *El Profesional de la Información*, 29(4), e290415. DOI: 10.3145/epi.2020.jul.15. 84

Thelwall, M., Bailey, C., Makita, M., Sud, P. and Madalli, D. (2019b). Gender and research publishing in India: Uniformly high inequality? *Journal of Informetrics*, 13(1), 118–131. DOI: 10.1016/j.joi.2018.12.003. 7, 84

Thelwall, M., Bailey, C., Tobin, C. and Bradshaw, N. (2019a). Gender differences in research areas, methods and topics: Can people and thing orientations explain the results? *Journal of Informetrics*, 13(1), 149–169. DOI: 10.1016/j.joi.2018.12.002. 7, 16, 84, 85, 86

Thelwall, M., Buckley, K., and Paltoglou, G. (2012). Sentiment strength detection for the social web. *Journal of the American Society for Information Science and Technology*, 63(1), 163–173. DOI: 10.1002/asi.21662. 27, 28

Thelwall, M. and Cash, S. (to appear). Bullying discussions in UK female influencers' YouTube comments. *British Journal of Guidance and Counselling*. 7, 97

Thelwall, M., Makita, M., Mas-Bleda, A. and Stuart, E. (2021). "My ADHD hellbrain": A Twitter data science perspective on a behavioural disorder. *Journal of Data and Information Science*, 6(1). DOI: 10.2478/jdis-2021-0007. 2, 7, 24, 91, 92

Thelwall, M. and Mas-Bleda, A. (2018). YouTube science channel video presenters and comments: Female friendly or vestiges of sexism? *Aslib Journal of Information Management*, 70(1), 28–46. DOI: 10.1108/AJIM-09-2017-0204. 6

Thelwall, M. and Mas-Bleda, A. (in press). How does nursing research differ internationally? A bibliometric analysis of six countries. *International Journal of Nursing Practice*. DOI: 10.1111/ijn.12851. 7, 87, 95

Thelwall, M. and Stuart, E. (2019). She's Reddit: A source of statistically significant gendered interest information? *Information Processing and Management*, 56(4), 1543–1558. DOI: 10.1016/j.ipm.2018.10.007. 7

Thelwall, M. and Thelwall, S. (2020). Covid-19 tweeting in English: Gender differences. *El Profesional de la Información*, 29(3), e290301. DOI: 10.3145/epi.2020.may.01. 6, 15, 75, 76, 77, 78, 79, 80

Thelwall, M. and Thelwall, S. (2021). Racism discussions on Twitter after George Floyd during Covid-19: A space to address systematic and institutionalized racism? Social Science Research Network. https://papers.ssrn.com/sol3/papers.cfm?abstract_id=3764867. DOI: 10.2139/ssrn.3764867.

Thelwall, M. and Thelwall, S. (submitted). Autism Spectrum Disorder on Twitter during Covid-19: Account types, self-descriptions and tweeting themes. 7

Thelwall, M. (2015). Evaluating the comprehensiveness of Twitter Search API results: A four step method. *Cybermetrics*, 18-19, p1. http://www.cybermetrics.info/articles/v19i1p1.html. 17

Thelwall, M. (2018a). Social media analytics for YouTube comments: Potential and limitations. *International Journal of Social Research Methodology*, 21(3), 303–316. DOI: 10.1080/13645579.2017.1381821. 6

Thelwall, M. (2018b). Can social news websites pay for content and curation? The SteemIt cryptocurrency model. *Journal of Information Science*, 44(6), 736–751. DOI: 10.1177/0165551517748290. 7

Thelwall, M. (2018c). Can museums find male or female audiences online with YouTube? *Aslib Journal of Information Management*, 70(5), 481–497. DOI: 10.1108/AJIM-06-2018-0146. 7, 49, 81, 83

Thelwall, M. (2018d). Gender bias in sentiment analysis. *Online Information Review*, 42(1), 45–57. DOI: 10.1108/OIR-05-2017-0139. 6

Thelwall, M., Thelwall, S. and Fairclough, R. (submitted). Male, female and nonbinary differences in UK Twitter user self-descriptions: A fine-grained systematic exploration. 6, 19

van Diepen, C. (2018). A Twitter-based study on the reach of a smoking cessation organization and the social meaning of smoking (Doctoral dissertation, University of Portsmouth). 15

Vicari, S. (2020). Is it all about storytelling? Living and learning hereditary cancer on Twitter. *New Media and Society*, 1461444820926632. DOI: 10.1177/1461444820926632. 13

Wang, G. (2018). A corpus-assisted critical discourse analysis of news reporting on China's air pollution in the official Chinese English-language press. *Discourse and Communication*, 12(6), 645–662. DOI: 10.1177/1750481318771431. 96

Wilkinson, D. and Thelwall, M. (2011). Researching personal information on the public Web: Methods and ethics. *Social Science Computer Review*, 29(4), 387–401. DOI: 10.1177/0894439310378979. 99, 100

Author Biography

Mike Thelwall, Professor of Data Science, leads the Statistical Cybermetrics Research Group at the University of Wolverhampton, UK. He has developed free software and methods for social media sentiment analysis and for systematically gathering and analyzing web and social web data. He is particularly interested in social science applications of web data. His program SentiStrength is sold commercially, given free to academics, and used in several academic social media analysis toolkits. He has co-authored hundreds of refereed journal articles and has written three books. He is an associate editor of the *Journal of the Association for Information Science and Technology* and sits on four other editorial boards.

CPSIA information can be obtained
at www.ICGtesting.com
Printed in the USA
FSHW021422220221
78733FS

9 781636 390659